The Portable Stanford

S0-BQY-525

published by the
Stanford Alumni Association

UNDER THE GUN provides an accurate and extraordinarily insightful history of U.S.-Soviet relations, presented in a manner which is compelling analytically, yet still delightful to read. Anyone with an interest in U.S.-Soviet relations, whether a specialist in arms control or a citizen with the most casual acquaintance with the subject, will enjoy and benefit from Coit Blacker's concise history of the great powers' relations. . . . This sort of integrated analysis is rare, and particularly notable because of the elegant and eminently legible style. UNDER THE GUN is a truly excellent book, well worthwhile for a wide range of readers.

Barry M. Blechman
Assistant Director,
U.S. Arms Control
and Disarmament Agency
1977–1979

Professor Blacker's book has the rare virtue of making the complex intelligible without oversimplifying either the Soviet-American relationship or the intricacies of the arms race and the arms-control process. While he has strong convictions—and makes them clear—he has the enviable capacity to view and describe the behavior of both sides with a good deal of detachment. The book thus gains greatly from the fortunate combination of competence and clarity, good sense and good style.

Alexander Dallin
Professor, History and
Political Science
Stanford University

UNDER THE GUN

Nuclear Weapons and the Superpowers

Coit D. Blacker

Stanford Alumni Association
Stanford, California

THE PORTABLE STANFORD is a series
publication of the Stanford Alumni
Association. Each book is an original
work written expressly for this series by
a member of the Stanford University
faculty. The PS series is designed to bring
the widest possible sampling of Stanford's
intellectual resources into the homes of
alumni. It includes books based on
current research as well as books that
deal with philosophical issues, which by
their nature reflect to a greater degree the
personal views of their authors.

THE PORTABLE STANFORD
Stanford Alumni Association
Bowman Alumni House
Stanford, California 94305

Library of Congress Catalog Card
Number 86-62853
ISBN: 0-916318-21-4

For Michael, Monica, and Mark

Series Editor: Miriam Miller
Production Coordinator: Gayle Hemenway
Cover Design: Dan Frazier

Contents

Acknowledgments

It is a pleasure to acknowledge the assistance and support of those individuals who, in one way or another, made this book possible. My greatest debt is to Miriam Miller, editor of The Portable Stanford series. That the book exists is a testament to Miriam's persuasive powers and to her outstanding editorial skills. *Under the Gun* is our first collaborative effort but not, I hope, our last. I am also indebted to Gayle Hemenway, series production coordinator, who devoted far more time and attention to this project than any author has a right to expect.

In my ten years at Stanford I have had the rare good fortune to have had some of this country's most distinguished scholars as friends and colleagues. In the Department of Political Science, Alexander Dallin, Alexander George, and Condoleezza Rice have been especially influential in the development of my thinking on U.S.-Soviet relations and the political and military dilemmas posed by nuclear weapons. During my time at Stanford, I have been most closely associated with the Center for International Security and Arms Control. Sidney D. Drell and John W. Lewis, the Center's directors, have contributed to my work in more ways than I can count. I am enormously grateful to them for their consistent support and encouragement.

For taking the time to read and critique the manuscript, I thank Barton Bernstein, Barry Blechman, Janne Nolan, and Condoleezza Rice. Without exception, their comments were focused, incisive, and thorough. The book is immeasurably better, in my judgment, for their having labored through it in draft. Philip Farley's comments were extremely valuable in sharpening and refining the central arguments in Chapter 4. For his tireless and all-around assistance—from working closely with me in the development of the book's central themes to the preparation of the endnotes—I extend my heartfelt thanks to Matthew State, who, in numerous ways, has contributed to most of my scholarly writings over the course of the last five years. Gratitude should not be confused with obedience. Although I am sincerely grateful to all the above for their advice, I did not always follow it. As a consequence, full responsibility for any errors of fact or judgment rests with me.

Finally, I want to express my appreciation to—and beg forgiveness from—those friends and family members who had essentially no choice but to tolerate my dark moods during the many months when the writing of the book occupied most of my waking moments. I apologize, in particular, to Louis Olave and Jay Chiles. While neither read a single page, both were forced, most often against their will, to listen to every sentence at least once.

Chronology

1945	*April*	Franklin Roosevelt dies; Harry Truman becomes 33rd U.S. president
	May	End of World War II in Europe
	July	Truman, Winston Churchill, and Josef Stalin meet in Potsdam
		"Trinity" atomic bomb test in Alamogordo, New Mexico
	August	Atomic bombings of Hiroshima and Nagasaki
		Japanese surrender
1947	*March*	Truman proposes U.S. military and economic assistance to Greece and Turkey (Truman Doctrine)
	June	Secretary of State George Marshall unveils U.S. program to rebuild West European economies (Marshall Plan)
1948	*February*	Communist takeover in Czechoslovakia
	June	Beginning of Berlin blockade
1949	*April*	Creation of the North Atlantic Treaty Organization (NATO)
	May	End of Berlin blockade
	August	Detonation of first Soviet atomic bomb
	October	Communist victory in China
1950	*June*	Outbreak of Korean War
1952	*November*	Dwight Eisenhower elected 34th U.S. president
		Detonation of first U.S. thermonuclear (fusion) device
1953	*March*	Stalin dies
	July	Korean armistice
	August	Detonation of first Soviet thermonuclear (fusion) device
1954	*January*	Secretary of State John Foster Dulles announces U.S. policy of "massive retaliation"
1955	*July*	Eisenhower meets in Geneva with Soviet leaders Nikita Khrushchev and Nikolai Bulganin
1956	*October–November*	Hungarian uprising and Suez crisis in Middle East
	November	Eisenhower elected to second term
1957	*August*	Soviets test first intercontinental-range ballistic missile
	October	Soviets launch Sputnik
1958	*Spring–Summer*	U.S., British, and Soviet "experts" meet to discuss issues involved in conclusion of a comprehensive nuclear test ban
	November	U.S., Britain, U.S.S.R. suspend atmospheric nuclear weapons testing (moratorium ends September 1961)

1959	*September*	Khrushchev visits U.S.; meets with Eisenhower
1960	*May*	U.S. U-2 spy plane shot down over Soviet territory
		"Big Four" summit collapses in Geneva
	November	John F. Kennedy elected 35th U.S. president
1961	*April*	Fidel Castro defeats U.S.-trained Cuban exiles in Bay of Pigs invasion
	June	Kennedy and Khrushchev meet in Vienna
	August	Construction of Berlin Wall
1962	*October*	Cuban missile crisis
1963	*August*	U.S., Britain, U.S.S.R. sign Limited Test Ban Treaty
	November	Kennedy assassinated in Dallas, Texas; Lyndon Johnson becomes 36th U.S. president
1964	*October*	Khrushchev overthrown; succeeded by Leonid Brezhnev (Communist Party general secretary) and Alexei Kosygin (prime minister)
1967	*June*	Johnson and Secretary of Defense Robert McNamara meet with Kosygin in Glassboro, N.J.
1968	*August*	Soviet and Warsaw Pact invasion of Czechoslovakia
	November	Richard Nixon elected 37th U.S. president
1969	*November*	Strategic Arms Limitation Talks (SALT) convene for first time in Geneva
1972	*May*	Nixon and Brezhnev, at Moscow summit, sign the Anti-Ballistic Missile Treaty and the Interim Agreement on Offensive Forces
	November	SALT II negotiations begin
1974	*August*	Nixon resigns as president; Gerald Ford becomes 38th U.S. president
	November	Ford and Brezhnev meet in Vladivostok; issue instructions for conclusion of new SALT agreement
1976	*November*	Jimmy Carter elected 39th U.S. president
1979	*June*	Carter and Brezhnev sign SALT II treaty in Vienna
	August	"Discovery" of Soviet combat brigade in Cuba
	November	U.S. embassy seized in Tehran
	December	Soviet Union invades Afghanistan
		Carter requests that Senate suspend consideration of SALT II
1980	*November*	Ronald Reagan elected 40th U.S. president
1981	*October*	Reagan administration unveils $180 billion program to modernize U.S. strategic military forces
	November	U.S., U.S.S.R. begin negotiations to limit intermediate-range nuclear forces (INF) in Europe
1982	*June*	U.S., U.S.S.R. begin Strategic Arms Reduction Talks (START)
	November	Brezhnev dies; succeeded by KGB chief Yuri Andropov

1983	*March*	Reagan proposes Strategic Defense Initiative
	November–December	U.S.S.R. breaks off INF and START negotiations
1984	*February*	Andropov dies; succeeded by Konstantin Chernenko
1985	*March*	U.S., U.S.S.R. resume arms control negotiations Chernenko dies; succeeded by Mikhail Gorbachev
	November	Reagan and Gorbachev meet in Geneva
1986	*May*	Reagan administration announces that U.S. will no longer be bound by the weapons limits contained in the unratified SALT II treaty
	July	U.S., Soviet negotiators meet in Moscow to explore possibilities for progress in arms control

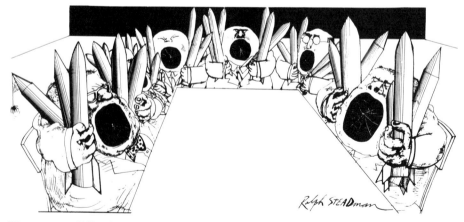

Disarmament Talks / *Ralph Steadman*

Getting Started

The destructive energy released by all the weapons of all the belligerent countries during the Second World War equaled some 3 million tons of TNT. That conflict, the most consumptive of human life in recorded history, began along the German-Polish border on September 1, 1939 and ended six years later in Tokyo Bay. Today, the nuclear weapons arsenals of the two superpowers contain something on the order of 18 billion tons of TNT. A single American submarine of the Trident class, armed with 24 missiles, carries within its hull the equivalent in destructive force of eight wars on the scale of World War II. Moreover, in the nuclear age the relevant measure of time has become minutes rather than years. Should the United States and the Soviet Union ever find themselves at war, thousands of nuclear weapons could be detonated in less time than it takes many Americans to commute to work.[1]

The statistics are sobering but also numbing. Most of us have heard them all before; the numbers simply reinforce what we already know. When we do think about our predicament, we concentrate our energies on trying to find a way out of it. We tend to focus on what needs to be done from this point forward in the understandable hope of leaving behind a safer world. It is vitally important that we persist in that effort but we also need to understand how and why we got into this situation in the first place. This book is about the impact of nuclear weapons on the character and the conduct of U.S.-Soviet relations since 1945. We all recognize that the two sets of issues— the invention and subsequent widespread deployment of nuclear weapons and the postwar rivalry between the superpowers—are intertwined, but the nature of that connection needs to be explored.

Is the political competition between Washington and Moscow responsible for the nuclear arms race or does the mere existence of these weapons drive the antagonism, imparting to it a special intensity? Or is some combination of the two at work, our political differences stimulating in both countries military responses that then feed back into the political process, setting off a never-ending cycle of "worst-case" military planning? One purpose of this book is to shed light on this interaction—to unravel its complexity and to provide the analytical tools to distinguish between cause and effect. If we are to have any real prospect of influencing the future in positive ways, it is critically important that we have a solid and informed understanding of the past.

The book begins with an analysis of the nature of U.S.-Soviet relations. Why don't Washington and Moscow get along? What are the sources of their antagonism? Some observers contend that any two great powers with such vastly different social and political systems as the United States and the Soviet Union are bound to compete, that confrontation is all but inevitable. Others disagree, alleging that the sharply adversarial nature of superpower relations since 1945 is largely the result of distrust and misperception. To what extent are ideology, cultural differences, history, and clashes in values responsible for perpetuating the U.S.-Soviet rivalry? In what areas do U.S. and Soviet interests overlap and how important are those shared goals? What kind of relationship should the United States seek with the Soviet Union? What is realistic, given the likely persistence of our deep differences?

These questions—and their answers—cannot be separated from what I've labeled in Chapter 2 "the nuclear revolution." What has been the impact of nuclear weapons on the military strategies of the United States and the Soviet Union? Most readers will be familiar with the term nuclear deterrence, but what does it actually mean? How has the concept changed over the last thirty years? What is its future?

It is one of the book's central propositions that nuclear weapons are different—radically so—and that coming to grips with that fact constitutes a necessary step in understanding the unique character of superpower relations after 1945 and in designing a strategy that will enable the two countries, in the words of arms control analyst Freeman Dyson, to "live and let live."[2]

Much of the study focuses on the on-again, off-again efforts of Washington and Moscow to limit their nuclear arsenals through negotiation, as well as their intermittent attempts to manage and improve their political relations. Chapters 3 and 4 examine the period we commonly call the Cold War—that is, the nearly two and a half decades bracketed by the end of World War II in 1945 and the Soviet invasion of Czechoslovakia in August 1968—when the superpowers made essentially no progress in limiting arms. Both chapters draw extensively on the work of such longtime observers of U.S.-Soviet political and military relations as Barton Bernstein, John Lewis Gaddis, George Kennan, George Quester, and Adam Ulam. Chapter 5 focuses on the years 1969 to 1980, a period in which the United States and the Soviet Union negotiated and concluded several important arms control agreements, including the 1972 Anti-Ballistic Missile Treaty and the Strategic Arms Limitation Treaty of 1979 (SALT II). Chapter 6 is devoted to an analysis of the Reagan administration's arms control and nuclear weapons policies. These last two chapters rely much less on existing scholarship and are woven together from my own work, some of which has been previously published.

The purpose of the final chapter is to offer some considered judgments about the future. In light of existing political conditions and predictable trends in technology, where are we and the Soviets likely to end up by the end of the century? Will the strong commitment of President Reagan to the development of strategic defenses, the so-called "Star Wars" initiative, enhance or diminish this country's security? Is the probability of war increasing or decreasing? Does negotiated arms control have a future?

This book is not a history of U.S.-Soviet relations. Nor is it a comprehensive study of the nuclear arms race and efforts to control it. Several dimensions of the arms control problem, including the possible spread of nuclear-weapons technologies to countries not now in possession of such capabilities, are not considered in detail. There are many excellent works on these subjects that treat more fully a number of issues that this book can only examine in a cursory fashion. A list of suggested readings is appended. It is, rather, a book on superpower relations and the peculiar, important, and often misunderstood role that nuclear weapons have played in shaping what most of us will agree has been the most profound international political rivalry of this or any other age. The book will have succeeded in its purpose less if it convinces than if it provokes those who read it to learn more about the issues that constitute its focus.

Illustration by Brad Holland

1 | Inescapable Rivalry

Since the defeat of Nazi Germany and Imperial Japan in 1945, the relationship between the United States and the Soviet Union has dominated American thinking about world affairs. We worry about other things, of course: relations between the United States and the countries of Europe, Asia, Africa, and Latin America; the widening economic gap between the rich nations of the First and Second Worlds, on the one hand, and the poor countries of the Third World, on the other; and the persistence of various regional conflicts, so destructive of human life and material resources, in such areas as southern Africa, Southeast Asia, and Central America. And yet, most of the images we carry with us when visualizing important world events have to do with the intense rivalry between the two superpowers.

Among the events and images of the last 40 years that stand out for their drama and intensity are the Berlin blockade of 1948-49; the grim presence of Josef Stalin in Red Square; the launching of Sputnik in October 1957; Nikita Khrushchev, shoe in hand, denouncing U.S. imperialism at the United Nations; the Cuban missile crisis; Richard Nixon and Leonid Brezhnev signing the first strategic arms limitation agreements in the Kremlin; and, more recently, the November 1985 summit between President Reagan and General Secretary Gorbachev in Geneva. Even the wars this country has fought since 1945—in Korea and Vietnam—are linked in American minds to the ambitions of the Communist leadership in Moscow. Try as we may to focus on other issues, our attention usually centers on the precise state of U.S.-Soviet relations and on the threat the Soviet Union is seen to pose to American national interests and to the American way of life.

Why do Americans worry so about the Soviet Union, a country with which the United States has never been formally at war and with which it was once allied? What is it about us—or them—that prevents us from thinking about much else when we ponder the state of the world and when we are asked to confess our greatest fears and anxieties? The obvious answer is that the two countries, the most heavily armed states in human history, have the capacity to destroy one another, and much of the rest of the planet, in thirty minutes. But our mutual hostility predates the acquisition of vast nuclear weapons arsenals. Something else must account for the suspicion and distrust that has characterized U.S.-Soviet relations since the Bolshevik seizure of power in Russia in November 1917.

A host of American "experts" on the Soviet Union and contemporary international relations, including scholars, diplomats, and senior political figures, have offered numerous and widely differing explanations for the enduring character of the antagonism between Washington and the Kremlin. Some seem not only unfounded but bizarre; others seem to come much closer to the mark, satisfying, at least for a while, much of our curiosity. Most capture elements of the truth, but few in the end leave us completely satisfied.

Four Images of the U.S.-Soviet Competition

Four schools of thought have been especially influential in shaping American attitudes toward the problem of U.S.-Soviet relations. The first constitutes what is often called the Realist school. The political scientist Hans Morgenthau, writing in the 1940s and 1950s, provided much of the intellectual architecture that underpins this interpretation.[1] Henry Kissinger, the man most responsible for the formulation and conduct of U.S. foreign policy during the Nixon and Ford administrations, and Zbigniew Brzezinski, President Carter's national security adviser, are two of its most influential exponents.

The Realist School

Realists start from the proposition that in the absence of a supreme authority, the international environment is essentially anarchic in character, so that the system resembles what the seventeenth century English political theorist Thomas Hobbes described as a "state of nature." Countries, as the largest and most powerful units within the system, are forced to compete with one another for their security and well-being. States prosper by either containing or defeating the ambitions of their rivals, or they become victims of the system, sometimes surrendering territory and population and at other times ceasing to exist altogether. Poland, partitioned three times between 1772 and 1795 by its more powerful neighbors, is an excellent example of this dynamic. In this Darwinian conception of international politics, only the strongest—or the best defended—survive.

Competition between states is seen as the usual, rather than the exceptional, state of affairs. When peace prevails, it is often a peace imposed or maintained by the most powerful state in the region, one strong enough to prevent disputes among smaller countries or to force a settlement when disagreements arise. At other times, peace can result from a balance of power among a group of countries, each roughly equal in strength, and none strong enough to prevail militarily over a coalition of its rivals. The absence of a general war in Europe between the Crimean War in the 1850s and the outbreak of World War I in August 1914 is typically thought of as a peace maintained through a balance of power.

But what fuels competition among states? A Realist would quite likely respond that a key factor driving a country to compete—to maximize its power—is distrust of its rivals. In some cases, such fear is warranted by historical experience. In the years between the First and Second World Wars, France struggled to keep Germany weak and to isolate it diplomatically, in large part because of the latter's invasion of France in 1914 and its four-year occupation of the northern third of French territory. In other instances, the fear seems misplaced or exaggerated. While the Soviet Union suffered tremendous losses as a consequence of Hitler's war of aggression, in no real sense does the Federal Republic of Germany today pose a threat to the security of the U.S.S.R. and yet the Soviets constantly warn of West German military ambitions, "revanchist tendencies," and the revival of Nazism.

Ambition also fuels international rivalries. Not all countries that maintain large armed forces do so for purely defensive purposes. At times, most states, great and small, have coveted the territory, resources, and populations of their neighbors. Sweden, for example, generally regarded as one of the most peace-loving countries of the modern era, was once an imperial predator of the first rank; similarly,

Figure 1-1 / Superpower Status – Who Has It?

	U.S.	U.S.S.R.
Area (square miles)	3,618,770	8,649,540
Population	239,600,000	276,500,000

GNP, 1983 (U.S. dollars in billions)	3,429.1	1,902.3

Defense expenditure as a share of GNP, 1983 (%)	6.1%	15%

Among countries not considered superpowers, China, Japan, and West Germany come closest to challenging the U.S. and the U.S.S.R. in terms of leading indicators of world power.

the westward expansion of the United States came at the expense of Mexico and the native American Indian population.

A Realist would tend, therefore, to assume a moderate to high degree of rivalry and competition between the United States and the Soviet Union as a result of the simple and unalterable fact that they are the two preeminent countries in the contemporary world. In political science terms, they are hegemonic states, each possessing large and capable populations, vast lands and resources, and impressive military capabilities. (See Figure 1-1.) In addition, each superpower has arrayed about it a collection of allies and clients who contribute to its power and status and in turn receive varying degrees of physical protection. The de facto division of the developed world into two camps since 1945—the liberal-democratic and the Communist—has tended to reinforce the imagery of "us versus them," which is seldom conducive to a process of accommodation and the easy resolution of disputes.

Reduced to its most elemental form, the Realist position is that the United States competes with the Soviet Union because the latter exists. Soviet interests are at some level bound to come into conflict with those of this country, even in ways that are at times difficult to

China	Japan	W. Germany
3,691,500	145,849	96,026
1,015,000,000	121,800,000	61,200,000
328.4	1,166.4	601.1

| 8.6% | 1.0% | 3.4% |

Sources: Population data (excluding China), The International Institute for Strategic Studies, *The Military Balance 1985–1986* (London: The International Institute for Strategic Studies, 1985); population data for China, *Asia 1984 Yearbook* (Hong Kong: Far Eastern Economic Review, 1984). GNP data (excluding China) and defense expenditure percentages (excluding U.S.S.R. and China), U.S. Central Intelligence Agency, *Handbook of Economic Statistics, 1985* (Washington, D.C.: U.S. Government Printing Office, 1985) GNP data for China, *Asia 1984 Yearbook*; defense expenditure percentage for China, U.S. Arms Control and Disarmament Agency, *World Military Expenditures and Arms Transfers 1985* (Washington, D.C.: U.S. Arms Control and Disarmament Agency, 1985). For the U.S.S.R., 15 percent is, within the U.S., the generally accepted estimate of defense spending as a share of GNP.

define precisely. As the only state with the means to threaten their existence, the Soviet Union arouses fear and distrust among Americans, just as the United States does among Soviet citizens. In such a setting, actions that one side takes to defend its interests are often perceived by the other as aggressive or offensive in character. Robert Jervis of Columbia University has written at length about this problem, which he and others have termed the security dilemma.[2]

A major weakness of the Realist school is its tendency to focus on the state as the central force in the international arena and to overlook the extent to which world politics is shaped by a variety of other factors that do not respect international boundaries—from religious differences and conflicts over ethnic self-determination to epidemics and food shortages. Another weakness is the implicit dismissal of the individual as a key actor in international affairs. People do make a difference, sometimes operating as a force for good and, at other times, generating extraordinary human suffering and material devastation. Some Realists have tended to underplay the fact that history is often made by particularly powerful or influential men and women, operating as either representatives or opponents of duly constituted political systems, and not exclusively by the disembodied entity we call the state.

Historical Determinism

A second school of thought is really a variation of the Realist model: Its proponents hold that the U.S.-Soviet competition is in some sense historically determined or, at a minimum, heavily shaped by a series of interconnected historical events. Historical Determinists, as they are sometimes called, part company with the Realists in that they pay less attention to the structure of international relations and more to the particular character of relations between the superpowers since the establishment of the Bolshevik regime. A more expressive way to say much the same thing is to argue that the United States and the Soviet Union got off to a bad start and that the two countries have never really recovered.

This thesis is certainly supported by the record. In portraying the coming to power of Lenin and his colleagues in the Russian capital of Petrograd (now Leningrad), in 1917, the *New York Literary Herald*, for example, wrote of various kinds of revolutionary excess, including sexual depravity and the wholesale destruction of churches, neither of which occurred, at least not in the spectacular fashion suggested by the newspaper. For a time in 1918 and 1919, the United States joined with British, French, and Japanese forces in an effort to topple the Bolshevik regime—a poorly considered and poorly executed invasion of Russian territory that left the new government deeply distrustful of and hostile toward the outside world. For their part, upon coming to power, the Communists repudiated Imperial Russia's considerable financial debt to Britain, France, and the United States, without which the Empire could not have undertaken its first concerted drive toward industrialization, leaving Western industrialists and financiers holding literally hundreds of millions of dollars in worthless paper.

The situation never improved very much as the years passed. In 1939, Western leaders condemned the non-aggression pact between Soviet Russia and Hitler's Germany, seeing it as a kind of unholy alliance which freed the Nazis to dismember Poland and then to unleash the Wehrmacht against the Low Countries and France without fear of Soviet reprisal. Later in the war, after the Soviet Union, having been attacked by the Germans in June 1941, had joined forces with the West, Stalin complained bitterly that the United States and Britain were delaying the opening of a "second front" in Western Europe in order to bleed Russia white.

There is, of course, merit to many of these and later charges hurled like invectives back and forth across the East-West divide. The purpose here is not to debate them but to consider their impact on the development of relations between the superpowers. Doubtless, the rocky start in relations did much to poison the subsequent history. One result of that initial antagonism was to set up a pattern of hostility that once established was difficult to arrest, let alone undo. Having come to expect animosity and bad faith, each side saw precisely these elements in the actions and policies of the other. Whatever the actual intention may have been, this interaction produced a destructive and persistent "echo effect," to borrow a phrase from University of Michigan political scientist Robert Axelrod.[3]

Could it have been otherwise? Could the United States and the Soviet Union ever have developed their relations on a less hostile footing? The obvious answer is "Yes, given different circumstances." But the point is moot, because the historical record cannot be rewritten. More importantly, what we and the Soviets do from this point forward is not determined in advance. True, neither we nor our opposites in the U.S.S.R. begin each day with the proverbial clean slate. All humans are products of both the immediate and the more distant past. American views of the Soviet Union are strongly influenced by our particular reading of historical events, but within these constraints we are free to make our own decisions and to chart our own course. Is an appreciation of the relevant history important to understanding why we and the Soviets don't get along very well? Of course. Do those experiences make it hard to change direction? Certainly. History does not, however, make it impossible for us and the Russians to alter the relationship. Leaders in both countries made such an effort in the late 1960s and early 1970s—admittedly without lasting success—and they will do so again in the future.

Cultural Determinism

A third and in some ways much more interesting school of thought looks to the distinct political cultures of the two countries to explain the adversarial nature of their relations. According to these Cultural Determinists, Russians and Americans find themselves at perpetual loggerheads, at least in part because they are unable to understand each other's civic traditions. Americans are said to value individualism, initiative, limited government, and the rough and tumble of the marketplace. We are often described in political terms as anarchistic and in economic terms as risk-takers. Americans place extraordinary emphasis on individual human liberties, as contained in the Bill of Rights. We are said to resist centralization and bureaucracy, and the encroachment of government into our private lives. Typically, Americans are portrayed as an optimistic people, confident that the future holds even bigger rewards, and supremely self-confident.

Many Western observers contrast these national traits with what they regard as the most salient features of the Russian political and economic experience. The Russian people, it is often alleged, are communal rather than individualistic in their orientation, more fearful of a weak government than a strong one, predisposed by history to value security more than opportunity, insular, suspicious of foreign influence, inured to violence, and prone to political excess. Democracy, it is occasionally pronounced with certainty, never took root in the autocratic Russian soil.

While there is something to these stereotypes, especially those that Americans hold about themselves, more often than not they are based on a cursory reading of history and on an understandable human urge to impose some kind of order on a mass of confusing detail. All of us try to tie up the loose ends, to find an explanation that permits us to unite the disaggregated bits of data we carry around with us in our heads. In the case of Americans viewing Russians and Russians viewing Americans, each side prefers to force an artificial unity by overlooking, omitting, or obscuring those elements that don't fit the analysis rather than settling for partial answers.

This is not to suggest that sharp differences in political cultures do not exist. Russian émigrés who have taken up residence in the United States frequently recoil at the chaos of American life; they complain, for example, that the people of this country, unlike ethnic Russians, have little collective identity, and express disbelief that in one of the richest nations in the world millions of citizens are homeless and unemployed. In much the same way, Americans who have traveled to the Soviet Union find the lack of spontaneity and the relative complacency of the population oppressive and depressing.

"Say, you are spoiling the view by standing there!"
(Sign reads: 5 million unemployed.)

This cartoon depicting American affluence side by side with high unemployment was originally published in *Krokodil*, the official Soviet humor magazine.

A common cultural experience and similar patterns of political development are not always essential, however, for the maintenance of correct if not cordial international relations. In some ways we Americans feel more of an affinity for China and the Chinese people than we do for many of the peoples of Western Europe, to whom most of us are more closely linked ethnically. This despite the fact that relations between the United States and the People's Republic of China could hardly have been worse in the years between the Communist victory over the Kuomintang in October 1949 and President Nixon's trip to Beijing in February 1972. The same holds for Japan. It is difficult to imagine two cultures with less in common than the Japanese and the American and yet we genuinely respect and admire our principal Asian allies. And, despite frictions over trade relations, the respect is mutual.

Finally, in the case of Russians and Americans, there is much each side finds attractive, even inspiring, about the other. Americans listen to and enjoy the music of the Russian masters. We read Dostoevsky and Tolstoy. We are moved by the obvious sensitivity of the Russian people and by their love of family. Russians identify with the restlessness and pioneering spirit of Americans, with our hubris and our sense of special mission. And they are deeply respectful of American economic achievements and technological prowess. There is, in short, much that draws the two peoples together. The distinct cultures of the United States and the Soviet Union do not make the two countries natural enemies. They simply make us different.

Americans should resist the temptation, in other words, to blame the generally dismal state of U.S.-Soviet relations on the many cultural, economic, and political differences that distinguish the two societies. To do so would be to reason selectively and to find answers where none exist. Diversity does not constitute a barrier to cooperation. It can, of course, and sometimes does. But it need not.

The Ideological Imperative

A fourth way of explaining the adversarial nature of U.S.-Soviet relations is to examine the very real differences in ideology that divide the two countries. That task is complicated by the fact that, unlike the Soviet Union, the United States has no official set of precepts offering guidance in virtually every area—from the setting of prices to the conduct of foreign policy—to which its leaders pay ritualistic homage. We have no leather-bound and gold-trimmed volumes incorporating the wisdom of Thomas Jefferson to compete with the Collected Works of V. I. Lenin. Americans, however, do have an implicit ideology, not unlike the British constitution—unwritten yet enormously important in influencing both the formulation and the implementation of foreign and domestic policy. ·

John Lewis Gaddis, the distinguished historian of postwar U.S. foreign policy, draws special attention to what he terms the "universalist" impulse in American diplomacy.[4] By that he means the extraordinary emphasis that U.S. leaders, from Wilson to Reagan, have traditionally attached to the realization of certain international goals that have their roots in the domestic American experience. Among these are political self-determination, anti-colonialism, representative democracy, and capitalist economic development. The universalist or liberal ideal also translates into opposition to totalitarian political forms, such as fascism and Communism, and economic autarchy and isolation. Woodrow Wilson's Fourteen Points, his plan for a just peace following World War I, is perhaps the best example of the attempt to put these principles into practice. Wilson failed, of course, and left office a sick and deeply disillusioned man.

More often than not, these precepts are left implicit and vague; to the extent that they inform U.S. policy they do so haphazardly. In addition, they offer little guidance for the conduct of diplomacy on a day-to-day basis. Most important of all, perhaps, they have been manipulated by policymakers to justify courses of action that, to be charitable, bear little resemblance to the ideal. U.S. support for authoritarian regimes is the most familiar example of the discrepancy between the vision and the reality, although given the antipathy of the universalist ideal to Communism, it is not all that difficult to explain.

The point, simply, is that while Americans don't often think of this country as having an ideology, at least not in the same sense that the term is used in reference to the Soviet Union, we do formulate foreign policy according to a loosely integrated set of principles and ideals, self-serving to be sure, that is expressive of how we see ourselves and how we want others to view us.

In contrast to the imprecision of the American belief system, Soviet ideology is explicit and formal. Marxism-Leninism, according to Moscow, is scientific socialism, an all-inclusive theory by which to explain the entire complex of political, economic, and social relations, both within countries and among them. At the heart of Soviet ideology is the idea that economics determines politics. Countries with capitalist economies, such as the United States, maintain bourgeois political forms, which, while democratic in appearance, are actually structured to perpetuate the power of the "exploiting classes"—in this case the capitalists and their toadies. Eventually, however, capitalism so exploits the workers, or the proletariat, that the impoverished rise up, destroy the old regime, and seize the means of production. The result, ideally, is a workers' state. Allegedly, the Soviet Communist party, as the most disciplined and politically conscious segment of the working class, constitutes its vanguard. Its purpose is both to defend the gains of socialism against counter-revolutionary forces and to guide the society toward the goal of "developed socialism."

In foreign policy terms, Marxist-Leninists view the world through the prism of the international class struggle, with the progressive forces, meaning the Soviet Union and its allies, in constant competition with the imperialists and their clients. Prior to World War II, the Soviets saw the British Empire as the most powerful element within the capitalist camp. Following the war, the mantle of imperialist leadership passed to the United States. During Stalin's years, Soviet propagandists held that war between the socialist and capitalist worlds was inevitable, a view that was not amended formally until Nikita Khrushchev's famous speech at the Twentieth Communist Party Congress in 1956. In addition to condemning the crimes of Stalin, Khrushchev proclaimed that, while a new world war between East and West remained a possibility, it could be prevented through adherence to the principles of "peaceful coexistence."

Khrushchev's amendment aside, Marxist-Leninists continue to attach central importance to this notion of the dialectic in international relations. It holds that economic and political competition between the two world systems is intense and pervasive and that, while the victory of socialism is assured, the struggle will be both long and dangerous.

Americans find this confrontational quality of Soviet ideology extremely threatening. It serves to underscore the idea of a rigid division of the world, a tense and potentially catastrophic split that leaves no gray area for compromise or accommodation. Soviet rhetoric, with its militaristic images and its emphasis on the life-and-death character of the competition, does little to ease American minds.

In practice—and this is often lost sight of—Soviet leaders have been cautious in their promotion of revolution, seldom challenging the United States in those areas of the world in which it has well-defined and important national interests. That the Soviets have been brutal in their suppression of autonomous tendencies within Eastern Europe is apparent. They have not, however, sought to extend the socialist revolution by force of arms to the countries of Western Europe (which may or may not be the result of the North Atlantic Treaty Organization, or NATO, the political and military alliance linking the United States to most of the countries of Western Europe, including the United Kingdom, France, and the Federal Republic of Germany). In Asia, the Soviets provided considerable material assistance to both North Korea and North Vietnam, but they did not involve themselves directly in the fighting with the United States and its allies during either of those wars. In the one instance in which the Kremlin did challenge the United States in an area of the world understood to be of vital interest to this country, namely Cuba in 1962, the Soviets retreated in the face of superior American power and resolve.[5] In those instances in which the relative power and interests of the two sides have been more nearly equal, as in the October 1973 war in the Middle East, both superpowers have acted with considerable restraint.

In the conduct of foreign policy, ideology serves a similar purpose for the United States and the Soviet Union. For both countries it provides a context for and often legitimizes either the threat or the actual use of force beyond their borders. For neither Washington nor Moscow, however, does ideology determine the circumstances under which power is actually employed in pursuit of national objectives. Typically, these decisions are made on the basis of prevailing conditions and near- to medium-term calculations of risk and gain. Soviet ideology is not a blueprint for the conquest or the subjugation of the non-Communist world, any more than the American vision constitutes a plan to liberate what we still term the "captive nations" of Eastern Europe. Ideologies are important devices for instilling certain values in the domestic population and for justifying to them the conduct of a specific foreign or military policy. The problem, of course, is that the other members of the international community listen in and may or may not take comfort from what they hear. Hitler, for example, was only too willing to communicate his megalomania to any and all audiences, internal and external. He consciously sought to legitimize German territorial ambitions by reference to the ideology of national socialism. But in no sense did the ideology compel Hitler to attack Poland in September 1939; he made that decision as an individual and not as a prophet of Nazism.

Americans take Soviet ideology so seriously precisely because of the experience of World War II. After the war, we came to equate Nazism and Communism, just as we came to equate Stalin and Hitler. Both forms of government are totalitarian in form and both, therefore, must pose the same kind of threat to American interests. It does not diminish the threat that the Soviet Union and Communism do pose to the United States and its allies to argue that Soviet ideology is different from its Nazi counterpart and therefore requires a different response. The Soviets are opportunistic in foreign policy— only too eager, it seems, to extend their influence to those areas where the benefits of doing so clearly outweigh the potential risks. For the most part, however, they have been unwilling to challenge the West when they perceive the danger of confrontation to be high. The Nazis, by contrast, were reckless, if not suicidal, in their pursuit of national glory.

The fact that Soviet ideology does not drive Kremlin decision makers to attack the United States offers some comfort but does not incline us to let down our guard. The collectivist goals of Marxism-Leninism, its devotion to the principle of one-party rule, and its intolerance of dissent, are repugnant to most Americans. Many Russians find American policies and practices no less disturbing. What gives the ideological competition its intensity, however, is the sheer size of the competitors. If Czechoslovakia were the only Marxist-Leninist state, Americans wouldn't pay much attention. Nor would the Soviets, if the sole liberal democracy were Ireland. It is the fact that Soviet ideology is wedded to a country with 280 million people and in possession of 25 thousand nuclear weapons that gives us pause. Would we fear the U.S.S.R. if it were not a Marxist-Leninist state? Probably much less than we do now, depending, of course, on what political system were instituted in its place. Would the United States and the Soviet Union still be rivals? Proponents of the Realist school would most likely respond in the affirmative. And chances are they would be right.

Toward a Synthesis

As interesting and intellectually provocative as these four efforts to explain the U.S.-Soviet rivalry may be, chances are that they still leave us with a lingering sense of dissatisfaction. For that, we should be grateful. It serves to remind us that answers to complex problems are seldom simple. If, however, we find none of these images fully convincing, how are we to develop a better, more subtle understanding of the superpower relationship?

The first step is to recognize that the relationship between Washington and Moscow does have many features of a traditional great-power rivalry. The Realists are correct in arguing that the bipolar structure of contemporary international relations contributes to the adversarial nature of the competition. While several other countries have larger populations and a few, such as Japan and West Germany, are important economic actors, only the United States and the Soviet Union merit the title of superpower. They are preeminent in world affairs to an extent that is without precedent in the modern era. Moreover, both have sought and continue to seek at least the maintenance, if not an extension, of their power and influence. There is, in other words, a willfulness to their behavior as hegemonic states that is frequently overlooked, especially when Americans and Russians consider their own conduct. Great powers become great because they possess the resources, the desire, and the skill to dominate their surroundings and to exercise leadership. When they lose that ability or suffer a loss of will, they cease being great powers—sometimes quite suddenly, sometimes over decades or centuries.

For countries such as the United States and the Soviet Union that exercise either control or influence in areas far beyond their borders, the mere existence of another state with roughly equal capabilities can be cause for concern if not anxiety. Actions that one country takes, ostensibly in defense of its position, a second country may interpret as threatening to its security, and vice versa. Late in the nineteenth century, for example, Britain and Russia eyed one another suspiciously across the mountains of Afghanistan. London suspected that St. Petersburg was eager to extend its influence to the Indian subcontinent and undertook to reinforce its garrisons guarding the northern approaches; Russia saw British actions as potentially aggressive in purpose and took steps to defend its southern borders. Each country, while believing that its own actions were purely defensive in character, acted in such a way as to exacerbate the fears and suspicions of its rival.

In the case of the United States and the Soviet Union, this structural predisposition to compete has been reinforced by a lengthy history of conflict over particulars: Greece in 1947, Berlin in 1948, Korea in

1950, Suez in 1956, and Cuba in 1962, to name only a few. These confrontations set up a pattern that has tended to make future clashes more likely. They are not, however, responsible for U.S.-Soviet hostility, as is sometimes imagined. The essentially antagonistic nature of the superpower relationship produces conflict, not the other way around. Americans care less, for example, about Angola than about Soviet influence in Angola. Nicaragua constitutes a crisis in American foreign policy not because it poses a threat to U.S. national security in any direct way, but because it has the potential to become a Soviet client.

The second step in advancing our understanding of U.S.-Soviet competition is to recognize that, while essential, an appreciation of the great-power aspects of the relationship takes us only so far. After all, the rivalry between Washington and Moscow is hardly unique; many other countries, admittedly less powerful, have challenged each other for political and military preeminence, either regionally or on a global scale. One of the factors that makes this relationship so different—and so intense—is ideology.

Each of the two superpowers—the Soviet Union self-consciously so—views itself as the principal exponent and primary defender of a distinct set of core values, applicable across international boundaries. Soviet ideology is explicit and highly formalized; the American vision is much less easily articulated and certainly less systematic.

The most important consequence of these ideological convictions and the passion with which they are held is to transform an already deadly competition between two heavily armed opponents into a contest between right and wrong, between good and evil. Americans resist not only the extension of *Soviet* power, but the spread of *Communism* wherever that danger is alleged to exist. Soviet leaders preach the mirror image of that message: that a vigilant struggle must be waged against both the United States and, more generally, the imperialist threat. Political authorities in both capitals would most likely agree with the assertion that the rivalry between the superpowers is at least as much a contest between two systems as it is a struggle between two countries.

Ideology tends, in other words, to undergird the division of the world into two parts. John Foster Dulles, President Eisenhower's Secretary of State, was notorious in his contempt for neutralism. He saw it as a form of political cowardice. For Dulles, the lines were clearly drawn and those who weren't America's friends were, by definition, America's enemies. The Soviets still stumble occasionally on the issue of neutralism, although since Khrushchev's time they have evidenced a much greater willingness to cultivate cooperative relations with countries pursuing a "non-capitalist path" of economic development, such as India. Despite having to adjust both their rhetoric and their policies, however, Moscow and Washington continue to interpret most global developments through the prism of bipolarity.

The danger in so doing is twofold. First, it promotes a simplified view of the world that can mislead policymakers. The Johnson administration, for example, justified American participation in the Vietnam War largely by reference to the aggressive aims of "international Communism," suggesting that Moscow and Beijing were somehow directly responsible for both the Viet Cong insurgency and North Vietnam's attacks against its southern neighbor. The effect was pernicious, as it led U.S. leaders to overlook the extent to which the war was a civil struggle that would have taken place with or without great power intervention. The Soviets appear to be making the same kind of mistake in Afghanistan, having convinced themselves that the United States and Pakistan, rather than popular resistance, are to blame for the problems of the Communist government in Kabul.

Second, bipolarity promotes a certain rigidity in thinking that can narrow the range of options considered by policymakers. The United States, for example, was slow to perceive the unraveling of the Sino-Soviet alliance in the late 1950s and even slower to explore how the split between Moscow and Beijing might enable this country to improve relations with both. The Soviet Union, for its part, initially resisted the diplomatic overtures of West German Chancellor Willy Brandt in the late 1960s directed toward a normalization of relations between Bonn and Moscow—overtures that eventually led to the conclusion of an entire series of mutually advantageous agreements between the Federal Republic of Germany and the countries of Eastern Europe, including the Soviet Union.

Far from decreasing in importance, the ideological competition between the superpowers seems to have grown more intense over the last several years, coinciding with the coming to power of the Reagan administration. However one feels about this development, it clearly represents something of a throwback to an earlier period in U.S.-Soviet relations, in which the ideological dimension of the rivalry occupied center stage. At a minimum, this intensification of the war of ideas has not facilitated an improvement in relations and, in the absence of a decision on both sides to tone down the rhetoric, is likely to exacerbate tensions further.

A third step in the process of sorting through the complexity of the superpower relationship is to appreciate the central role of perception—or misperception—in decisionmaking.[6] Political leaders are subject to the same errors in judgment that afflict other mortals. The potential for misreading an adversary's intentions or for misinterpreting his actions is an ever-present danger. The leadership's access to expertise and to sensitive intelligence information may reduce the likelihood of a costly mistake but it does not, by any stretch of the imagination, eliminate that possibility altogether.

Two examples serve to illustrate this point. When the North Koreans attacked South Korea in June 1950, the Truman administration interpreted this assault as a Moscow-directed feint to the east, half expecting a Soviet invasion of Western Europe to follow. Over the next two years, the member countries of NATO, led by the United States, undertook a significant expansion in their military capabilities. Had Washington had access to better intelligence, however, it would have known that the Soviet Union was in no position in 1950 to unleash a general military assault against the West. Twelve years later, in the fall of 1962, Khrushchev sanctioned the deployment in Cuba of intermediate- and medium-range nuclear missiles in the expectation that President Kennedy, whom the Soviet leader regarded as untested and indecisive, would accept this change in the military status quo rather than risk a confrontation. Khrushchev's misreading of the President was costly in more ways than one from the former's perspective. Not only did it bring the world close to the brink of nuclear war, it was also politically costly for the General Secretary, contributing to his downfall in October 1964.

Compounding the very real problems in U.S.-Soviet relations posed by structure, history, and ideology is the tendency of decisionmakers on both sides of the political divide to misunderstand the words and actions of their adversaries, producing a kind of multiplier effect. Awareness of the fact that humans perceive events selectively—that ultimately they see what they want to see—should induce caution as we look toward the future. Having come to expect hostility and deceit from Moscow, Americans are prepared to hear little else. The Soviets, of course, return the favor.

Would the problems end if Americans and Soviets were suddenly able to see each other with pristine clarity? As this discussion has suggested, at the root of the competition are fundamental differences between the two sides that would persist, whether or not their analytical powers were to improve. The rivalry is not, as sometimes alleged, the consequence of a simple misunderstanding. What might change, however, were we better equipped to discern each other's motives and to read each other's actions, would be the ability to distinguish between genuine and imaginary threats to national security. It is unlikely in the extreme that by so doing Americans and Russians would grow to like each other, but at least we might learn to fear one another a little less.

U.S.-Soviet relations are not some gigantic jigsaw puzzle, waiting to be solved. The leaders of our two countries cannot fix the relationship, as a mechanic might repair an automobile. There is no easy solution to this central problem of our time, a problem that has been with Washington and Moscow since 1917 and that will persist for as long into the future as any of us can see. Relations between countries—be they allies or adversaries—can only be managed. When international relationships are managed well, violent conflicts can be avoided and at least some kinds of cooperation encouraged. When they are managed poorly, the result is often war. By this standard, the United States and the Soviet Union haven't done all that badly, although whether the two sides have been skilled or just lucky is difficult to say. If we and the Soviets are to maintain this uneasy truce, however, both of us must resist the temptation to be done with the problem one way or the other and strive, quite simply, to become better managers—keeping in mind that the most likely alternative to this strategy is a nuclear war which neither side can win and for which neither is even remotely prepared.

Endless War / *Wangdon Lee*

2 | The Nuclear Revolution

On July 16, 1945, near Alamogordo, New Mexico, the United States successfully tested the first atomic device, code-named Trinity. Upon witnessing the explosion, J. Robert Oppenheimer, the scientific director of the wartime Manhattan Project, recalled the phrase "I am become death, destroyer of worlds," from the epic Sanskrit poem, the *Bhagavad Gita*. Four years later, on August 29, 1949, the Soviet Union detonated a comparable weapon. We have no reliable record of what Oppenheimer's Soviet counterpart, I. V. Kurchatov, said or thought on that occasion, although he is reported to have been intensely relieved that America's nuclear monopoly had been broken.

Today the United States and the Soviet Union each possess approximately 10,000 long-range nuclear weapons targeted against each other's military forces, industrial facilities, and communications centers, many of which are located in or near urban areas. Together, the two countries also have something on the order of 30,000 shorter-range nuclear weapons, most of which are deployed with ground, sea, and air forces in and around Europe and the Far East. In the forty years since that first Trinity test, the superpowers have built enough nuclear weapons to inflict catastrophic destruction on each other's societies, as well as to devastate much of the rest of the world, in thirty minutes. Never before in its long history has the human species held such awesome power in its hands. In response to this unprecedented situation, Robert McNamara, Secretary of Defense during the Kennedy and Johnson administrations, once remarked that "there is no longer any such thing as strategy, only crisis management."[1]

The invention and widespread deployment of nuclear weapons constitutes the single most important development in military history. Other weapons breakthroughs have been significant, yet none can be compared, even remotely, to the nuclear revolution. The genius of humankind has provided the world with countless ways to inflict death on the battlefield, from crossbows to poison gas, but only in the last half of the twentieth century has it produced what have come to be called weapons of mass destruction.

It has been conservatively estimated that in the event of a large-scale nuclear exchange between the superpowers, 100 million American and Soviet citizens could perish in the length of time it takes to drive from San Francisco to the campus of Stanford University, thirty-five miles to the south. Deaths caused by the delayed effects of blast, fire, radiation, and exposure could equal or exceed that number in the space of a month. An epidemic spread of disease and severe genetic abnormalities would very likely afflict those in the targeted areas who survived the initial attack. The poisoning of the atmosphere, the water supply, and the soil could pose serious and long-term health hazards to people living hundreds if not thousands of miles from the scenes of the greatest devastation. Beyond a certain threshold, the use of nuclear weapons might also induce what has been described as the "nuclear winter effect," in which the incineration of combustible materials could generate thousands of tons of ash and soot; carried aloft by winds, these pollutants might then form a thick and persistent cloud cover, reducing the surface temperature of the planet by several degrees. The impact on the agricultural cycle alone could be cataclysmic.[2]

The facts are plain enough. And yet we resist the reality. We convince ourselves that a nuclear war is a remote possibility and that even if one occurs it might be less terrible than we've been led to believe. We press our scientific and technical communities to develop reliable means to defend us against the effects of these weapons. We demand either more or fewer bombs to make us more secure. We realize at a gut level that nuclear weapons have done something profound to the character and the conduct of U.S.-Soviet relations, and to the prospects for humanity's survival, but we are not sure precisely what.

Coming to grips with the nuclear revolution requires a basic understanding of how nuclear weapons work and of their awesome destructive capacity, as well as some knowledge of how these weapons would reach their targets in the event of war. Most important, however, is a thorough appreciation for the fact that nuclear weapons have had an enormous impact on traditional military thinking and on the very concept of national security. This chapter is devoted to a consideration of these issues.

Some of the discussion that follows may strike those who have only a passing acquaintance with the terminology of the nuclear arms race as excessively detailed. To minimize confusion, I have sought to explain the relevant terms and concepts as directly as possible and to avoid excessive use of acronyms. Some readers may find even this level of detail distracting, but I urge them to press on. The material introduced in this section of the book is intended to inform and enrich the analysis that follows.

The Development of Nuclear Weapons

The nuclear weapons first tested by the United States and the Soviet Union in 1945 and 1949, respectively, were "fission" or atomic devices, so called because they derived their explosive power from the splitting of such heavy isotopes as uranium 235 and plutonium 239. To make such a bomb, a chain reaction of splitting atoms must be sustained through many "generations." If this reaction can be contained for a sufficient time within a given space, the ultimate result is a sudden release of energy that dwarfs any attained with conventional chemical explosives. Prior to the advent of atomic weapons, a bomb weighing, say, one thousand pounds could produce a destructive yield roughly equivalent to the same amount of TNT. A fission weapon, on the other hand, can generate a yield several thousand times its own weight. The bomb the United States dropped on Nagasaki on August 9, 1945, tipped the scales at approximately 10,000 pounds, yet its destructive force was equal to 40 million pounds of TNT, or, as it is more often expressed, 20 kilotons. The yield-to-weight ratio of this particular weapon was thus 4,000 to 1 (20,000 tons to 5 tons).

The destruction wrought by the atomic bombing of Japan was enormous. In Hiroshima, four and one-half square miles of the city were flattened; at least 65,000 people were killed and 70,000 injured. While the famous fire bombings of Dresden and Tokyo during World War II took more lives, it is important to remember that hundreds of aircraft, depositing thousands of weapons, participated in those attacks, which stretched over several days. The 250,000 casualties in Hiroshima and Nagasaki were inflicted in a matter of seconds.

Development work on the bomb continued after the war. By 1952 the United States was able to detonate fission weapons with an effective yield of 500 kilotons, roughly 25 times as powerful as the bomb used against Nagasaki. Moreover, by the early 1950s, the U.S. stockpile of weapons had grown to more than one thousand. In the Soviet Union, work was proceeding at a comparable pace, although the American program was more advanced technically.

From Fission to Fusion

Also in 1952, the United States successfully tested the first thermonuclear, or hydrogen, device. Unlike *atomic* bombs, which obtain their explosive power from *fission*, *thermonuclear* weapons are products of the *fusing* of hydrogen nuclei. Fusion can only occur, however, in the presence of tremendous heat and pressure. With the development of the atomic bomb, scientists for the first time had the practical means to create such conditions. Using a fission device as a trigger, the United States was able to fuse deuterium (a hydrogen isotope) to form helium, creating in the process an explosion roughly equivalent to 10 million tons of TNT or 10 megatons. The first hydrogen device, code-named Mike, was therefore almost one thousand times as powerful as the weapon dropped on Hiroshima (13 kilotons). The Soviet Union detonated a similar weapon in November 1955, although it had tested a much smaller thermonuclear device in August 1953.

The development of the hydrogen bomb generated great controversy in American political and scientific circles. In January 1950, largely in response to the detonation of the first Soviet atomic bomb the previous summer, the Truman administration decided to proceed with plans to build the weapon—despite a recommendation, submitted by the General Advisory Committee of the U.S. Atomic Energy Commission on October 30, 1949, that the United States not do so. The GAC, made up of many of the most prominent scientists and technologists involved in the atomic bomb project, argued that, given the ongoing advances in fission weaponry, the "super" was unnecessary for the defense of the country. In a separate document submitted the same day, six GAC members, including Oppenheimer, expressed their views with extraordinary bluntness:

We base our recommendation on our belief that the extreme dangers to mankind inherent in the proposal wholly outweigh any military advantage that could come from this development. Let it be clearly realized that this is a super weapon; it is in a totally different category from an atomic bomb. The reason for developing such super bombs would be to have the capacity to devastate a vast area with a single bomb. Its use would involve a decision to slaughter a vast number of civilians. We are alarmed as to the possible global effects of the radioactivity generated by the explosion of a few super bombs of conceivable magnitude. If super bombs work at all, there is no inherent limit in the destructive power that may be attained with them. Therefore, a super bomb might become a weapon of genocide.[3]

Over thirty years later, this passage still serves to highlight the dramatic difference between fission and fusion weapons—a point not always appreciated in the public debate over nuclear weapons and the strategies for their use. Atomic (or fission) bombs could be justified in military terms as highly efficient and effective tools to accomplish a particular set of objectives in the event of war. While many times more destructive than conventional explosives, they were not seen to pose a threat to human survival. Hydrogen (or fusion) bombs are and were understood to be different. While they, too, could be used militarily, the fact that a single thermonuclear weapon could level an entire city and vaporize much of its population raised the spectre of an annihilating, genocidal conflict between the superpowers. Later weapons tests simply confirmed the suspicion. In 1961, for example, the Soviet Union tested a hydrogen bomb with an estimated yield of 58 million tons of TNT. Today, most of the nuclear weapons in the arsenals of the superpowers are fusion, not fission, devices, with yields ranging from several kilotons to 20 megatons. The worst fears of the six GAC scientists, so clearly expressed in their single-page letter to Atomic Energy Commission Chairman David E. Lilienthal in October 1949, would appear to have been realized.

Getting the Weapons to Their Targets

Keeping pace with these developments in weaponry were advances in the means of delivery. In the late 1940s and early 1950s, the

United States relied on a relatively small force of medium-range B-29 and B-50 bombers, as well as the longer-range B-36, to deliver its atomic weapons against the Soviet Union in the event of war. These were replaced by the first all-jet medium bomber produced in the United States, the B-47, and, beginning in 1956, by the first of the intercontinental-range B-52s. American industry built 1700 of the former and over 600 of the latter in a little over a decade. During the same time period, the Soviet Union developed a much smaller and less capable force of long-range aircraft, including two types of bombers with the ability to strike the United States from bases in the U.S.S.R. The Kremlin also built several times as many bombers for use against potential adversaries in Europe and Asia.

Intercontinental Ballistic Missiles (ICBMs)

Arguably, the most significant development of the nuclear age, other than the invention of the bombs themselves, occurred in August 1957, when the Soviet Union successfully tested the first ballistic missile of intercontinental range. Two months later, Moscow used the same type of missile to place into orbit the first artificial satellite, Sputnik I. Additional Soviet launches of a similar character followed in quick succession.

The Soviet breakthrough was important for two reasons. First, it strongly suggested that the Kremlin's long-range missile program was much farther along than its American counterpart. Second, and even more troubling to the people of this country, it meant that the Soviet Union could attack the United States with missile-launched weapons in the space of thirty minutes. By contrast, bombers taking off from U.S. bases still required up to ten hours to reach their destinations in the U.S.S.R.—although attacks could also be mounted from American overseas installations located much closer to Soviet territory. In light of the fact that ballistic missile warheads travel at more than 20,000 feet per second, it was immediately understood that the United States had no way to defend itself against an attack of this kind. Fears of a "missile gap" ensued, reaching their zenith during the 1960 presidential campaign between then Senator John F. Kennedy and Eisenhower's vice president, Richard Nixon.

As it turned out, the Soviet advantage was more apparent than real. By the time Kennedy assumed office in January 1961 the United States already enjoyed a lead in the number of deployed intercontinental-range ballistic missiles (ICBMs), a lead that was to widen appreciably over the next several years. Moreover, the Soviet Union did not construct hundreds of these first-generation long-range missiles, as originally predicted by some U.S. intelligence agencies. In fact, it was revealed years later that they never deployed more than a handful of these relatively crude rockets, known in the West as the SS-6. Rather than invest heavily in a program that suffered from a number of operational shortcomings, the Kremlin chose to cut its losses and concentrate on the development of the next generation of systems, which were procured in significant numbers after 1962.

From the Soviet perspective, a particularly unfortunate consequence of that decision—which may have been well-advised on technical grounds—was to place the U.S.S.R. in a position of strategic military inferiority at the time of the Cuban missile crisis in October 1962. The greater than four-to-one U.S. advantage in ICBMs at the time of that confrontation undoubtedly contributed to Khrushchev's willingness under pressure to dismantle the 42 medium- and intermediate-range missiles then being deployed on Cuban soil. Khrushchev's central purpose in deploying the weapons, of course, had been to reduce the numerical disparity in deployed missiles that had developed between the United States and the Soviet Union since the late 1950s.

By 1967 the United States had deployed 1054 ICBMs in underground concrete- and steel-reinforced silos. Since 1982 the number of missiles has actually decreased slightly, as the U.S. has begun to dismantle the oldest and least reliable of these systems (the 54 Titan IIs). The Soviet buildup did not really get under way until 1963-64 and did not level off until the mid-1970s. At the time of the signing of the first strategic arms limitation agreement (SALT I) in 1972, the Soviet Union maintained a force of approximately 1530 deployed ICBMs, with an additional 90 installations under construction. From a high of 1618 in 1975, the number of deployed Soviet ICBMs dropped to 1398 by 1979, in keeping with one of the provisions of SALT I. Roughly 60 percent of the Soviet missiles are essentially new delivery systems built since 1975, replacing older, 1960s-vintage weapons.

Submarine-Launched Ballistic Missiles (SLBMs)

In addition to manned bombers and ICBMs, both superpowers have constructed large fleets of submarines equipped with ballistic missiles. These SLBMs—submarine-launched ballistic missiles—are smaller, less accurate, of shorter range, and typically less destructive than land-based systems. Between 1960 and 1967, the United States

Soviet Delta III class ballistic missile submarine.

commissioned 41 Polaris-class submarines, each with 16 launch tubes, for a total of 656 missiles. In 1971, a completely new missile system was procured for the Polaris boats. The newest American ballistic missile submarine is the Trident, each of which is currently armed with 24 Trident I missiles. To date, eight have been deployed; twelve more are planned, to be introduced as the older submarines are retired from service. These extremely powerful weapon systems patrol vast areas of the world's oceans. While under way, they spend virtually all of their time under water, beyond the reach of surface vessels and patrol aircraft, making them all but invulnerable to attack by hostile forces.

The Soviets have built most of their modern ballistic missile submarines since 1968. They also operate more of them than the United States—62 versus 36 in late 1986—and have a correspondingly greater number of sea-based missiles. On the other hand, more American submarines and missiles are within range of their targets at any given time, although this pattern could change within the coming decade. Finally, Soviet submarines tend to patrol in waters much closer to home, enabling the Kremlin to offer them some protection against U.S. anti-submarine activities. Such deployment patterns are essential for these vessels, as they are easier to track and therefore to destroy than their more elusive American counterparts.

As of late 1986, the United States maintained a combined force of approximately 1900 long-range bombers, ICBMs, and SLBMs; the Soviet total is closer to 2500. Collectively, these are known in the jargon of the defense and arms control communities as strategic nuclear delivery vehicles. These figures do not include the intermediate-range ballistic missiles of the two superpowers, consisting of roughly 600 Soviet missiles targeted on Europe and Asia and 108 U.S. Pershing IIs based in Germany; the several thousand "tactical" aircraft capable of carrying nuclear weapons; or the nuclear-capable artillery tubes, deployed with U.S. and Soviet ground forces. Also not considered "strategic" are the naval vessels of the two sides— other than ballistic missile submarines—even though many of them carry nuclear weapons on board for possible use against enemy submarines and surface ships.

Weapons vs. Systems

While each of the superpowers targets roughly 10,000 nuclear warheads on the human and material resources of the other side, the number of strategic weapons obviously exceeds the number of strategic weapons systems, such as bombers and missiles. The confusion need not detain us for long. In 1970, the United States began to replace a portion of its single-warhead ICBM force with new Minuteman III missiles, each equipped with three weapons. Within certain geographic parameters, each of these new warheads can be directed to a different target. Weapons so deployed are known as MIRVs, standing for "multiple independently-targetable re-entry vehicles." The term is also used as an adjective (as in a "MIRVed missile"), and a verb (as in "we are MIRVing"). In addition to the 550 Minuteman III ICBMs, the United States deployed almost 500 MIRVed submarine-launched missiles in the early 1970s, replacing an equal number of older missiles equipped with only one weapon each. As a consequence, in several years, the number of U.S. ballistic missile warheads increased from slightly more than 1700 to about 7000, while the number of ICBMs and SLBMs remained constant. (For a comparison of U.S. and Soviet ICBM and SLBM deployments, including warheads, see Figures 2-1 and 2-2.) Typically, the MIRVed weapons are both more accurate and of a lower yield than the warheads they have replaced.

The Soviet Union undertook a similar modernization in the mid-1970s. Because Soviet land-based missiles are considerably larger than American ICBMs and therefore able to lift more payload, the Kremlin placed three times as many warheads on that part of its strategic arsenal as the United States did—up to ten, for example, on the largest of its missiles, the SS-18. On the other hand, the Soviets have MIRVed fewer of their submarine-launched missiles. In total, the Soviet Union is believed to have over 9000 ballistic missile warheads currently deployed.

The long-range bomber forces of each superpower are also being modernized. The United States, with approximately 250 such aircraft, places much greater emphasis on this leg of the nuclear triad (land-based missiles, submarine-based missiles, and bombers), than does the Soviet Union (see Table 2-1). American bombers are equipped with three types of nuclear weapons: gravity bombs, short-range attack missiles, and cruise missiles.

Modern cruise missiles are small, remotely piloted vehicles that fly extremely close to the ground at subsonic speeds. Their great

Figure 2-1
U.S. and Soviet SLBM Launcher Deployment and Warhead Totals, 1969–1985

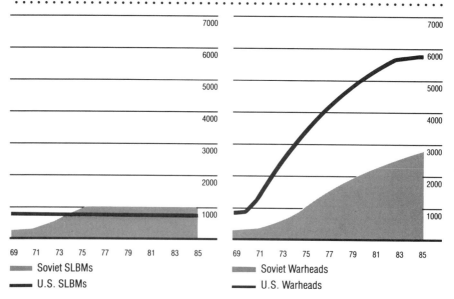

Increases in both countries' warhead stockpiles can be attributed mainly to the replacement of single-warhead missiles by missiles equipped with multiple independently targetable reentry vehicles (MIRVs).

advantage is that they can be launched while the bomber is still hundreds of miles from its target, beyond the reach of the enemy's air defense forces. This serves to enhance greatly the survivability of the bomber, while at the same time permitting it to carry out its military mission. In addition, cruise missiles are very difficult to locate and destroy because of their extremely small radar cross-sections, making it all but impossible for enemy radars to track them successfully. The United States was the first to deploy modern air-launched cruise missiles in the early 1980s; Soviet deployments began several years later.

U.S. cruise missiles also come in ground- and sea-launched versions. Four hundred sixty-four of the former are scheduled for deployment in Europe by 1988; several hundred of the latter will be carried aboard surface ships and submarines by the end of the decade. By far the greatest number, however, are being assigned to the bomber force—perhaps as many as 3000. The Soviet cruise missile program is expected to be more modest in scope, owing to the fact that the Kremlin maintains fewer bombers in its active inventory;

Figure 2-2
U.S. and Soviet ICBM Launcher Deployment and Warhead Totals, 1969–1985

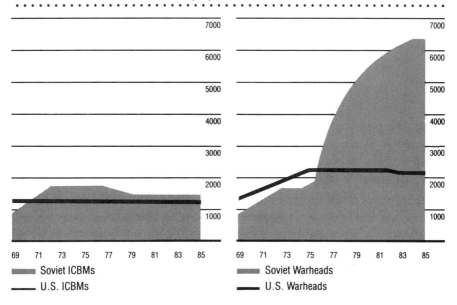

Source: Both Figures 2-1 and 2-2 were adapted from Department of Defense, *Soviet Military Power 1985* (Washington, D.C.: U.S. Government Printing Office, 1985).

Table 2-1 / Features of the "Legs" of the U.S. Strategic TRIAD

Intercontinental Ballistic Missiles (ICBMs)

- high degree of accuracy
- excellent command and control
- highest degree of reliability
- quickest reaction time
- lowest degree of "survivability"

Submarine-Launched Ballistic Missiles (SLBMs)

- highest degree of "survivability"
- highly resistant to detection and attack (while at sea)
- more tenuous communication links
- lower accuracies (but improving rapidly)

Long-Range Bombers

- high "survivability" of forces on alert (30%)
- recallable after takeoff
- slow flying
- vulnerable to air defenses
- most accurate

Source: Adapted from Thomas B. Cochran, William M. Arkin, and Milton M. Hoenig, *Nuclear Weapons Databook, vol. 1: U.S. Nuclear Forces and Capabilities* (Cambridge, MA: Ballinger Publishing Co., 1984).

U.S. strategic nuclear weapons are delivered by three principal means, each of which has relative advantages and disadvantages in terms of accuracy, responsiveness, reliability, and survivability.

moreover, several cruise-missile technologies, such as miniaturized turbo-fan engines, present special obstacles to Soviet industry.

Both superpowers continue to modernize their strategic nuclear arsenals. The United States, for example, will soon take possession of the first of 100 B-1 bombers. The B-1, cancelled during the Carter administration, was revived during President Reagan's first year in office. It is designed to supplement the aging (but still quite capable) force of B-52 aircraft, many of which will be retired from service within the next decade and a half. An even more sophisticated air-craft, the so-called "Stealth" or advanced technology bomber, is slated for deployment in the mid-1990s. Fifty MX or Peacekeeper ICBMs, each armed with 10 MIRVed warheads, will replace an equal number of Minuteman III missiles by late in this decade. The United States also may procure a small, single-warhead land-based missile, nicknamed Midgetman, after completion of the MX deployment. Beginning in 1989, a new submarine-launched ballistic missile of great accuracy, the Trident II, will be placed aboard all Trident submarines. Each Trident II missile is expected to carry eight independently-targetable warheads.

The Soviets have already begun to field a new single-warhead ICBM, their first such missile in ten years. A system very much like the American MX will begin deployment by the end of 1986. Several additional land-based missiles are under development, including a replacement for the largest Soviet ICBM, the SS-18. A similar momentum characterizes the Soviet SLBM program. Finally, a new long-range bomber, code-named Blackjack in the West, will probably enter regular production between now and the end of the 1980s. (See Figure 2-3 and Tables 2-2 and 2-3 for a comparison of U.S. and Soviet strategic nuclear forces in 1986.)

Strategic Defense

Rounding out the strategic military capabilities of the two superpowers are their respective strategic defense programs. For reasons explored more fully in Chapters 6 and 7, acquiring forces to defend one's self against nuclear attack provokes considerable controversy among some segments of the U.S. national security community. From the early 1970s to the early 1980s, the United States devoted relatively little attention and few resources to the strategic defense mission. This country has no effective defense against a Soviet nuclear attack, whatever the means of delivery, nor is any such defense likely to materialize in the foreseeable future.

The Soviet Union, on the other hand, has invested many billions of rubles in an effort to defend the territory of the U.S.S.R. against an attack by U.S. bombers. Estimates of the utility of these air defense forces vary widely. The Soviets also maintain a small force of anti-ballistic missiles (ABMs) arrayed around Moscow, designed to offer at least some protection against missile strikes, as well as an active and well-funded ABM research and development program. The Moscow system is limited in scope by the 1972 ABM Treaty with the United States, which severely restricts the deployment of such weapons on both sides. The Soviet ABM is thought to have little value against even a modest American attack, although it might prove effective in defending Moscow against a small force of missiles launched either accidentally or by design. It might also be of some

Figure 2-3 / Comparison of Superpower Nuclear Weapon Systems in 1986

ICBMs	U.S.S.R.	1396
	U.S.	1017
SLBMs	U.S.S.R.	979
	U.S.	640
Long Range Bombers	U.S.S.R.	170
	U.S.	241

Table 2-2 / Strategic Forces of the Soviet Union, 1986

Strategic weapon	Number	Number of warheads	Yield or weapons load	CEP* (meters)
Land-based missiles (ICBMs)				
SS-11 mod 1	28	1	950kt	1,400
mod 2/3	420	1	1mt	1,100
SS-13 mod 2	60	1	750kt	1,800
SS-17 mod 3	150	4	750kt	450
SS-18 mod 4	308	10	500kt	250
SS-19 mod 3	360	6	550kt	300
SS-25	70	1	550kt	200
Total	**1,396**			
Submarine-launched ballistic missiles (SLBMs)				
SS-N-5	39	1	1mt	2,800
SS-N-6	336			
mod 1		1	1mt	1,300
mod 2		1	1mt	1,300
mod 3		2	500kt	1,300
SS-N-8	292			
mod 1		1	1mt	1,500
mod 2		1	800kt	900
SS-N-17	12	1	1mt	1,400
SS-N-18	224			
mod 1		3	200kt	1,400
mod 2		1	450kt	900
mod 3		7	200kt	900
SS-N-20	60	9	100kt	500
SS-N-23	16	n.a.	n.a.	n.a.
Total	**979**			
Long-range bombers				
Tu-95 Bear	125		40t	
Mya-4 Bison	45		20t	
Total[e]	**170**			

Table 2-3 / Strategic Forces of the United States, 1986

Strategic weapon	Number	Number of warheads	Yield or weapons load	CEP* (meters)
Land-based missiles (ICBMs)				
Titan II	17	1	9mt^a	1,300
Minuteman II	450	1	1–2mt	370
Minuteman III	250	3	170kt^b	350
	300	3	335kt	220
Total	**1,017**			
Submarine-launched ballistic missiles (SLBMs)				
Poseidon C-3	304	10	40–50kt	450–550
Trident C-4	336	8	100kt	450
Total^c	**640**			
Long-range bombers				
B-52G	151		45t^d	
B-52H	90		45t	
Total	**241**			

Sources: *The Military Balance, 1985–1986,* International Institute for Strategic Studies (London, 1985) and *Soviet Military Power 1986* (Washington, D.C.: United States Government Printing Office, 1986)

*CEP: Circular error probable is a statistical measure of accuracy. If a missile is said to have a CEP of 300 meters, military planners are confident that if 10 warheads were released toward a target, 5 of them would land within a distance of 300 meters from that target. Accordingly a highly accurate missile has a low CEP.

^{a} mt: megaton
^{b} kt: kiloton
^{c} Deployed on 37 submarines
^{d} t: ton
^{e} Deployed on 77 submarines (940 SLBM and 62 subs are considered strategic under SALT counting rules; remaining subs and missiles are in theater role.)

limited value in blunting a Chinese, British, or French nuclear strike against the Soviet capital.

The possible utility of Soviet anti-ballistic missile systems is less important for our purpose than their mere existence. Along with the elaborate Soviet air defense network, it underscores the Kremlin's continuing interest in developing ways to lessen the impact of a nuclear war on Soviet society, industry, and war-making potential. The leadership's assignment of several billion rubles a year to support civil defense activities is consistent with this objective. Given the likely scale of destruction in any major nuclear war, many American strategic analysts tend to discount the effectiveness of such a program, which includes provisions for either the sheltering or the evacuation of urban populations. For better or worse, in the 1960s the

United States reached the conclusion that all such efforts were pointless. The Kremlin, while fully aware of the magnitude of the problem, decided otherwise.

The United States is now reconsidering its earlier decision. As a consequence of President Reagan's "Star Wars" speech of March 1983, this country has undertaken an expensive research effort—known as the Strategic Defense Initiative—to determine whether and under what conditions it might be desirable to deploy strategic defenses on such a scale as to afford meaningful protection to the American, and perhaps allied populations, against a Soviet missile attack. It will be some time before the United States is in a position to assess the practicality of such a program. Should this country determine that full-scale deployment of strategic defenses is warranted on technical grounds, however, the military and arms control implications will be profound.[4]

The nuclear arms competition between the United States and the Soviet Union, now stretching over forty years, arouses intense passion. Some regard it as the inevitable result of the political and military rivalry between the superpowers. Others see it as the direct consequence of a kind of technological imperative: Any weapon that *can* be built *will* be built. A third explanation looks to the so-called "military-industrial complex" in the United States and to what has been characterized as a "military-bureaucratic complex" in the Soviet Union as the driving force of the arms race. Finally, there are those who perceive the competition as a stupendous and avoidable mistake, brought on by a reinforcing cycle of misunderstanding and misperception, that has more to do with the suspicions and insecurities of political leaders in both countries than with any predetermined historical, economic, or technological factors. All would agree, however, that the nuclear revolution has transformed the nature both of war and international politics. This transformation—more fundamental and pervasive than most of us realize—warrants closer examination.

Nuclear Weapons and Military Strategy

The primary purpose of any country's armed forces is to defend the state against outside aggression. Military power can be used for other, less benign purposes, of course, ranging from coercion of neighboring countries to outright aggression. Great powers, like the United States and the Soviet Union, also deploy armed forces to safeguard various far-flung political, military, and economic interests that they regard as crucial to their well-being and to the maintenance of their status as first among equals within the international community. For most countries, including the superpowers, however, the enduring justification is defensive: to deter and, if the need arises, defeat any attack against the territory, population, and material resources of the state.

Historically, the most reliable way for a country to defend itself against the appetites of its neighbors has been through a combination of defensive and offensive military capabilities. When a country is attacked, the first two objectives are to deny the enemy its immediate military objectives and to limit the amount of damage that it is able to inflict. During this initial stage of hostilities, military forces geared to defend are of greater importance to the side being attacked than are offensive capabilities. Once the enemy assault has been contained, the victim then seeks to carry the war to the territory of the aggressor, both to disrupt the latter's war-making potential and to punish it. It is at this stage of the conflict that the defender's offensive forces assume a central role.

During the Second World War, for example, the entire Soviet war effort between the first day of the Nazi assault in June 1941 and the battle of Stalingrad during the fall and winter of 1942-43 was defensive in character: to halt the German attack and to keep as much Soviet territory, population, and industry as possible out of enemy hands. Only when the German advance had been checked were Soviet forces able to seize the strategic offensive. Fighting along the Western front followed a similar pattern. Critical to allied success was the ability to exhaust the German offensive through defensive military action. Once that task had been accomplished, the Western allies were in a position to bring their greater military and economic resources to bear and to engage in sustained offensive military operations. The result, as we know, was the complete defeat of the Axis powers in Europe and the Pacific.

Nuclear weapons play havoc with this traditional military logic. Because of the enormous destructive power of these weapons and the inability to defend effectively against a ballistic missile attack, neither the United States nor the Soviet Union has the capacity to protect—in any meaningful way—either its population or its industrial base. Classic notions of defense in such a situation lose much of their meaning.

Because neither side can reliably defend itself against nuclear weapons, both must look to a different mechanism to deter attack.

This they have sought to do by deploying at least a portion of their strategic nuclear forces in such a way that they cannot be destroyed in a preemptive strike. These weapons can then be used in retaliation, to inflict a level of destruction that the aggressor would regard as "unacceptable." In the early 1960s, Secretary of Defense Robert McNamara determined that the ability to cause the prompt deaths of 25 percent of the Soviet population and to destroy 50 percent of that country's industry in retaliation was sufficient to deter any intentional Soviet nuclear attack.

Nuclear Deterrence

This is the essence of nuclear deterrence: that U.S. and Soviet security depends, in the final analysis, not on either side's ability to "win" a nuclear war by any recognizable definition of that term but on the riveting reality that both sides would surely lose, independent of who struck first or the success of that initial attack. Nuclear deterrence, then, is less a policy than it is a condition. In a very real sense, we hold the Soviet population hostage to the actions of its leaders, and vice versa. It is an unprecedented situation that leaves us, and we assume our Soviet counterparts, frustrated, fearful, and more than a little depressed.

In our military policy, we vacillate between accepting the logic of mutual deterrence and seeking to undo it. During the latter part of the Kennedy administration, for example, Defense Secretary McNamara embraced, after some reluctance, the idea of "assured destruction" as the most reliable guarantee of peace in the nuclear age. He argued that given the growth in U.S. and Soviet nuclear weapons stockpiles since the late 1940s and the vulnerability of the two sides to retaliation, neither could hope to prevail militarily over the other. Moreover, any attempts to acquire such war-winning capabilities were likely to end in failure, as the other side could simply keep pace. Procuring additional nuclear weapons made little sense. In any event, nothing could be done to shield the aggressor from the catastrophically destructive counterblow that would inevitably follow any first strike. For all its drawbacks, McNamara reasoned, the balance of terror made an intentional nuclear war between the superpowers a remote possibility.

Not all American strategists have found McNamara's logic convincing. According to some of these analysts, the most effective way to deter a Soviet attack is by having the capability to prevail in the event of war. The key to such a strategy is the capacity to limit damage to the United States. There are two ways to pursue this objective: through strategic defense (developing the means to defend American territory against Soviet nuclear weapons) and through counterforce targeting (acquiring U.S. offensive forces that are themselves able to locate and destroy Soviet weapons before they can be used). The fact that neither a viable strategic defense nor a completely effective "disarming" first strike is possible at this time does not prevent those who hold these beliefs from pressing their case.

No U.S. administration has pursued either strategy—assured destruction or damage limitation—to the exclusion of the other. Complicating matters is the fact that there has never been complete agreement, either within particular administrations or between successive ones, about what types of weapons are needed to deter a nuclear attack on any scale, from an all-out assault to a limited strike, as well as to carry out a policy of assured destruction. The debate has centered on the realization that not only must the United States have the means to destroy the Soviet Union in retaliation for an extensive attack but that we must also make the Soviets believe that we have both the capability and the will to respond appropriately to any level of nuclear provocation. This emphasis on "limited nuclear options" and Soviet perceptions has opened up a Pandora's box of questions concerning what types of nuclear forces and what number are necessary to ensure that the threat of retaliation is credible.

As a consequence of these competing conceptions of strategy, the United States has ended up with an odd mix of nuclear forces. Some, such as the submarine-launched ballistic missiles, are ideal retaliatory weapons but of limited value for a first strike, as they currently lack the accuracy to destroy Soviet land-based missiles, secure in their underground silos. Others, including the multiple-warhead Minuteman III and MX missiles, do have the requisite degree of accuracy for these so-called counterforce missions, but at the present time the United States has too few of them to eliminate the entire Soviet ICBM force in a first strike. In any event, some fraction of the Soviet ballistic missile submarine force would surely escape destruction, enabling Moscow to retaliate against U.S. cities with hundreds if not thousands of nuclear weapons.

The apparent confusion in American nuclear strategy and in the standards by which we acquire our strategic forces is not exclusively of our own making. It is, at least in part, a consequence of Soviet behavior. The Soviet Union has deployed 40 percent more long-range

Lift-off of a Minuteman III missile. First deployed in 1970, 550 Minuteman IIIs constitute the backbone of America's land-based strategic nuclear forces.

ballistic missiles than the United States. It also, and more importantly, has equipped its ICBMs with more than enough high-accuracy warheads to destroy a large percentage of this country's land-based missiles in their silos. As we have already noted, the Soviet Union's investment in offensive nuclear forces has been accompanied by a companion effort in strategic defensive weaponry, including anti-ballistic missile installations around Moscow and defenses against manned bombers. Taken together, these activities strongly suggest that Soviet political and military leaders continue to resist the logic of assured destruction and seek the ability to limit the amount of damage the U.S.S.R. would sustain, should deterrence fail. This, in turn and not unreasonably, arouses suspicions in the United States that at least some in the Soviet Union believe it possible to fight and win a nuclear war.

To disabuse the Soviet leadership of any such notions, successive U.S. administrations have authorized both improvements in existing weapons, such as equipping bombers with cruise missiles, and the procurement of new systems in order to ensure that under any and all conditions American forces can retaliate effectively. At the same time and amid greater controversy, the United States is also seeking to place a high proportion of Soviet nuclear forces at risk, just as they have done to our Minuteman missiles, through the deployment of such advanced weapons as the MX ICBM and the Trident II SLBM, both of which will have the capability to attack the entire panoply of Soviet military targets, according to the Department of Defense.

The kind of deterrence described by former Defense Secretary McNamara does not require these kinds of capabilities; on the contrary, targeting the adversary's nuclear weapons only compels him to increase the size of his arsenal and to diversify how these forces are based in order to complicate the plans of the attacker. When both sides pursue such strategies, which is the case today, the result can be an arms race.

The irony, of course, is that neither side is likely to find itself any more secure in a competition of this kind. The stockpiling of additional offensive nuclear forces may increase the amount of damage that the Soviet Union is able to inflict on the United States in a first strike, but it is unlikely to decrease significantly the effectiveness of the American response, given the high proportion of U.S. forces that would "survive" such an attack. The reverse also holds true.

Ultimately, deterrence works because neither the United States nor the Soviet Union is currently in a position to defend or otherwise protect its cities—not because one side enjoys an advantage in the number of ICBMs, SLBMs, or bombers. Beyond a certain point, passed years ago, the raw numbers don't matter all that much. What does matter is that each side possesses enough weapons—even after being attacked first—to reduce the other side to rubble. It is for this reason that the U.S.-Soviet nuclear balance, once characterized as

U.S. B-1 bomber. The first 15 B-1s became operational in October 1986.

delicate, is anything but. The concept of "assured destruction" may make our blood run cold but it has served to deprive the Soviet Union of any possible incentive to initiate a nuclear exchange. If any American officials have ever entertained comparable ambitions, it has done the same. Macabre it may be, but deterrence has helped to maintain peace between the superpowers for forty years.

Nuclear Weapons and the Conduct of the Superpowers

The potentially catastrophic consequences of a nuclear war involving the United States and the Soviet Union have made policymakers in both countries extremely cautious, on balance, in the conduct of foreign policy. Although we have no way of knowing, it is entirely possible that in the absence of these weapons, Washington and Moscow might have come to blows years ago. During the Berlin crisis of 1961, for example, U.S. military forces might have intervened in an effort to prevent Soviet construction of the wall that today divides the former German capital, which, according to the postwar agreements governing its status, was to be administered as a single entity. That the United States took no direct action to challenge the Soviet move undoubtedly had something to do with the fear in this country that a military confrontation over Berlin could quickly escalate, possibly precipitating a general war in Europe in which nuclear weapons might be used.[5]

Caution is not a word we often hear in connection with U.S.-Soviet relations; on the contrary, the image is usually one of two great states, competing for power and influence, barely able to contain their hostility. The risk of war is seen to be ever present. Without diminishing the very real dangers implicit in the superpower competition, it is a fact that in their conduct—leaving aside their rhetoric—generally both sides have exercised prudence and restraint.

What is the evidence for this assertion? Let's begin with the way the United States and the Soviet Union talk about their vital national interests. Both have been extremely clear, on balance, in communicating what areas of the world, in addition to their own territory, they are prepared to defend by resorting to force. Through the mechanism of the North Atlantic Treaty, the United States pledges to regard an attack against any of its fifteen European allies as a de facto declaration of war against itself. Three hundred thousand American troops based in Western Europe anchor that commitment. We have similar defense arrangements with Japan, the Republic of Korea, Australia, and much of Latin America. Through the Warsaw Treaty Organization, the Soviet Union promises to defend Bulgaria, Czechoslovakia, the German Democratic Republic, Hungary, Poland, and Rumania against "imperialist aggression." Far from seeking to hide or deny these commitments, both superpowers have been eager to make them explicit in order to prevent misunderstandings that could lead to conflict. The predictable consequences of a nuclear war have led the United States and the Soviet Union to abandon subtlety in their alliance commitments. When they draw their lines in the dirt, they do so with firmness and announce it in a loud voice.

At the same time, so as to diminish the anxiety of its adversary, each superpower defines its commitments as defensive in character. Words do not always coincide with deeds, of course. The NATO allies view the Soviet military posture in Europe as decidedly offensive in nature, Moscow's declarations to the contrary notwithstanding. Western charges aside, the avowed purpose of Soviet and East European forces is to *defend* the socialist camp against a NATO assault. The West defines the role of its forces in Europe the same way, only in reverse—to deter a Communist attack.

Superpower caution has been manifested in yet a third way. With one notable exception, neither has directly challenged what are understood to be the central interests of the other. There has been no shooting war between East and West in Europe since the division of the continent at the close of World War II. When the Hungarians revolted against Soviet rule in 1956, the West, despite pleas to do so, did not intervene on the side of the "freedom fighters," at least in part because of the perceived risks. When the Chilean military overthrew Marxist President Salvador Allende in a violent coup d'etat in 1973, the Soviet Union did nothing beyond protesting his ouster. For the Kremlin, Chile was an interesting sideshow, but given American interests and military power in the region, hardly worth a confrontation with the United States.

The most dramatic exception to this pattern of restraint, of course, was the Cuban missile crisis, which ended ignominiously for the Soviet Union. The episode is a curious one for several reasons. First, it was a deliberate bid, without precedent in the postwar period, to change the military status quo between the superpowers. Second, it came at a time of overwhelming U.S. strategic nuclear advantage. Third, it took place in an area of the world in which the United States enjoyed conventional military superiority. Khrushchev may have gambled, based on the apparent unwillingness of the United States to oust Castro by direct application of force, that Washington would accept the missile deployments rather than fight. In 1962, Cuba fell into a kind of political nether world: No longer a part of the Western community, neither was it yet a full member of the socialist camp. Whatever Khrushchev's calculation, his decision cost the Soviet Union dearly in terms of prestige. It also provoked the most intense crisis in U.S.-Soviet relations in the history of the Cold War.

The disinclination of the superpowers to contest each other's vital interests has not prevented them from engaging one another militarily in less direct ways. U.S. military assistance to Israel and Soviet support for the Arab cause is perhaps the most familiar example. Despite the intensity of the fighting, however, in neither the June 1967 nor the October 1973 wars in the Middle East did either superpower intervene militarily on behalf of its client(s). When the Soviets threatened to do so at one point during the latter crisis, the United States made clear its opposition and the Kremlin reconsidered. Although a superpower mini-crisis ensued, the interesting fact is that both Moscow and Washington stepped back from the brink rather than risk a confrontation that could have gotten out of hand. The key to success in this instance was the willingness of the United States to press Israel to honor an earlier cease-fire agreement which, if left to collapse, could have resulted in the military rout of Egypt, at that time a Soviet client.[6]

The Middle East is but one area of the world in which the United States and the Soviet Union have found themselves on opposite sides of the same conflict; in none of these situations, however, have American and Soviet military forces ever engaged one another directly. That record is no accident. It attests to the great caution that has regulated the military conduct of the two superpowers when they have found themselves in face-to-face competition.

At various times, each side also has supplied arms and economic assistance to a country that finds itself at war with the other superpower. During the Korean and Vietnam wars, the Soviets supplied Pyongyang and Hanoi with billions of dollars' worth of military and economic aid, even though in both cases the principal antagonist was the United States. On a much smaller scale, Washington continues to lend assistance to the Afghan rebels in their struggle to free their country from Soviet military occupation.

What constitutes acceptable behavior in such instances is difficult to determine. But in the strange political and military game that has developed between the United States and the Soviet Union, the rule appears to be that as long as the conflict does not occur in an area of the world in which either or both superpowers have clearly demarcated and longstanding vital national security interests, such proxy involvement on the part of one superpower is permissible—even if the other superpower has already committed combat forces. The closer the contested area comes to constituting a vital interest, however, and the greater the level of proxy assistance, the more dangerous the game becomes. The absence of *overt* U.S. military assistance to the Afghan rebels is no oversight.

The real danger, of course, is that in one of these "gray area" conflicts, both countries might decide to deploy forces, with all the risks that might entail. Pertinent to the avoidance of such an incident is the thirty year on-and-off effort of the United States and the Soviet Union to elaborate what we might call "rules of the road" for the conduct of their relations. That the two sides have even made such attempts is a testament to the dramatic impact of nuclear weapons on postwar international politics.

Before nuclear weapons, adversarial states seldom sought to cooperate in the development of norms to guide their behavior. And when they did, as in the Concert of Europe system created in the aftermath of the Napoleonic Wars, the effort was often short-lived or never very effective to begin with. In the past, intractable political differences were usually resolved by resort to force. Going to war may have been costly in human and material terms but it was a singularly effective way to settle international disputes.

For the United States and the Soviet Union, nuclear weapons have dramatically reduced the range of military options. Both have had to rely more heavily on diplomatic and political mechanisms to compose their differences than would have been the case had these weapons never been invented. The objective need to do so, however, has not made the task any easier, as American and Soviet interests—and consequently their relations—remain fundamentally adversarial.

The result of this dynamic is predictable enough: from President Eisenhower's meeting with Soviet leaders Bulganin and Khrushchev in 1955 to the Reagan-Gorbachev summit thirty years later, the two superpowers have attempted every several years to discuss at the highest levels the entire range of international problems on which they disagree, though generally without much success. At times, as during the heyday of detente between 1971 and 1974, they have also tried to elaborate certain shared "principles of relations" designed to serve as a kind of road map to delimit the most dangerous aspects of their rivalry and to foster greater cooperation.[7] Invariably, however, such positive upturns have been followed by a worsening of relations, as the two countries find themselves at odds over some important issue or event. The 1955 "Spirit of Geneva," for example, was soon eclipsed by the Kremlin's nuclear threats directed against the United Kingdom and France at the time of the 1956 crisis over the Suez Canal. The detente of the early 1970s was followed by the most intense deterioration in relations since the period after the Cuban missile crisis—and it has lasted much longer.

Unwilling to go to war except for the most vital of interests and yet unable to eliminate through negotiations the tensions that make them adversaries, the superpowers vacillate between trying to get along and trying to get a leg up. They talk, argue, posture, threaten, and only occasionally agree. They solemnly acknowledge their responsibility to exercise restraint in the conduct of their relations while at the same time seeking to exploit one another's vulnerabilities and temporary political setbacks. They negotiate on the limitation of armaments, even as they accuse each other of violating virtually every international agreement to which the other is a party. Each has amassed military forces able to extirpate its opponent, although neither, it seems, has seriously contemplated the use of those weapons against its rival.

In short, nuclear weapons have led to a kind of paralysis in superpower relations that not only limits the circumstances under which Washington and Moscow might actually employ military force in the service of political goals, but also the very way in which they define and pursue their foreign policy objectives. Nuclear weapons don't facilitate the conduct of superpower diplomacy, they complicate it. They afford the United States and the Soviet Union less rather than more latitude in their mutual relations. For decisionmakers in both countries, nuclear weapons have been more of a curse than a blessing, their importance as the very symbol of what it means to be a superpower notwithstanding. Moreover, this condition is certain to persist for as long into the future as any of us can predict.

The nuclear revolution is only forty years old and yet it has radically changed our thinking about military power and political purpose. U.S. security, once based on our physical ability to protect all that we hold dear, now relies on our capacity—as well as our perceived willingness—to avenge even the most "dedicated" or determined nuclear attack. Reduced to the essentials, we may not be able to win a nuclear war, but we can surely guarantee that the Soviet Union can't either.

This sobering reality, which we and the Soviets would prefer to deny, forces each side to pursue a relatively circumspect course internationally, whatever the rhetorical flourishes that often accompany our respective foreign policy pronouncements. If there is a recurring theme in the U.S.-Soviet competition, it is our mutual caution, not our proclivity to excess; the number of times we and the Russians have found ourselves at the precipice of war can be counted on the fingers of one hand. In the jargon of American political scientists, the two sides have been "risk averse." The central question, of course, is, Will this pattern endure? The four chapters that follow, which focus on the character of the U.S.-Soviet nuclear weapons competition from 1945 to the present, attempt to answer that question. By better understanding what has come before, we can perhaps more effectively influence what lies ahead.

Peace '85 / *Tadahiko Ogawa*

3 | Uneasy Truce 1945–1955

The Truman Doctrine, the Marshall Plan, and the Communist coup in Czechoslovakia; the Korean War, massive retaliation, and Eisenhower's New Look; the Hungarian uprising, Sputnik, the missile gap, and the U-2 incident; the Bay of Pigs, the Cuban missile crisis, the Limited Test Ban Treaty, and the war in Vietnam. Together, these themes, events, and crises defined an age. We labeled it the Cold War and even now, 20 years later, the period evokes a powerful and well-defined set of historical images for those who lived through it. Something short of a real war and much less than the comprehensive peace we or our parents anticipated in 1945, the Cold War was a new and deeply disturbing experience that left Americans and their government frightened, frustrated, angry, and anxious. Always anxious.

That we—and our Soviet counterparts—felt this way should come as no surprise, especially in retrospect. The advent of nuclear weapons changed the character of the postwar competition between the United States and the Soviet Union in ways no one could have anticipated. Not only did these weapons make the U.S.-Soviet rivalry more dangerous than any that had come before, but their very existence seemed to feed our mutual hostility. The lingering sentiment in the United States to seek a resolution of our differences with the Soviet Union through negotiation—evident, for example, in the speeches and commentaries of 1948 Progressive Party presidential candidate Henry A. Wallace—vanished in 1949 as Moscow exploded its first atomic bomb.

To further complicate matters, we began to confuse cause and effect. We began to believe that in some indefinable way nuclear weapons were responsible for the Cold War. We and the Soviets must be enemies, we convinced ourselves. Why else do the two sides target each other's cities with weapons of mass destruction? We had it backwards, of course. The nuclear arms race was and remains the military expression of the deep political differences that divide the United States and the Soviet Union. While the weapons came to symbolize the adversarial nature of U.S.-Soviet relations, providing a focus for our fears, in no sense did they create the underlying conditions which gave rise to the postwar rivalry between the superpowers. Our confusion was regrettable, if unavoidable, as it complicated the efforts of policymakers and analysts to get at the root causes of the Cold War. We spent so much time worrying about the military competition—a justifiable preoccupation—that we tended to forget why we were in it in the first place.

American policy toward the Soviet Union from the late 1940s to the late 1960s reflected this confusion. On the one hand, having concluded by the spring of 1947 that the Kremlin posed no less a threat to U.S. security than had Nazi Germany and Imperial Japan during World War II, the Truman administration adopted a strategy to limit Soviet power to those areas then under the effective control of the Red Army. Termed "containment," this policy looked to a system of alliances and to American military superiority, especially this country's preponderance in nuclear weaponry, to ensure its effectiveness and credibility.

On the other hand, as early as 1946—and continuing sporadically throughout the next twenty years—the United States tried without much success to negotiate with the Soviet Union various measures, first to eliminate and later to control, the further growth and development of our respective nuclear weapons arsenals. That, implicitly at least, the containment policy relied on the maintenance rather than on the negotiated elimination of U.S. military superiority was an inconsistency of which few Americans—except those in government—were ever consciously aware. The fact that we couldn't have it both ways, Truman-style containment of the Soviet Union and disarmament, didn't stop us from thinking of both as central elements in U.S. policy. In practice, the former took precedence, suggesting that the American commitment to negotiate an end to the nuclear arms race from the late 1940s to the mid-1960s was more cosmetic than real.

The Soviet Union's Cold War policies were more consistent, although not without their own internal contradictions. The Kremlin pursued two fundamental and parallel objectives in the first twenty years after the defeat of the Axis powers. The first was to consolidate what Soviet leaders referred to as the postwar gains of socialism. Having created by force of arms a community of Communist states in Eastern Europe (while at the same time annexing territory at the expense of four of those countries), the Soviets were determined to secure what they had won. In the period immediately following the war, it was less than apparent that they would be able to do so, in light of America's nuclear monopoly and manifest economic superiority. Their second objective, therefore, was to acquire the means to deter direct American military action against the U.S.S.R. or its satellites. It was for this reason, among others, that Stalin ordered a crash program to develop Soviet nuclear weapons shortly after the atomic bombings of Hiroshima and Nagasaki. However absurd it may sound to American ears, fear of a U.S. attack—or, at a minimum, attempts by the United States to extract political concessions from the Kremlin through nuclear blackmail—provided the rationale for many Soviet military programs of the 1950s and 1960s.

At the same time, Soviet leaders routinely emphasized their devotion to "general and complete disarmament." Given the necessary link between the U.S. policy of containment and the maintenance of American military superiority, however, the Soviets could not have had much confidence that Washington would agree to such proposals, whatever the content of the official rhetoric. Nor would the Kremlin, were the situation reversed. Great powers do not lightly surrender military advantages, especially advantages of the kind and degree enjoyed by the United States during much of the Cold War. Thus, even as they berated successive American administrations for their refusal to ban the bomb, Soviet leaders were issuing instructions to their scientific and technological communities to expand, diversify, and improve the U.S.S.R.'s nuclear weapons stockpile.

The natural tendency is to conclude that each side cynically manipulated the disarmament issue in order to score propaganda points and embarrass its adversary. On one level, such was surely the case.

On a second and more subtle level, however, governments in both countries were attempting to respond to a completely novel situation that carried with it tremendous risks. As a consequence, U.S. policy sought to move in two directions simultaneously: the preservation of military superiority and the negotiated reduction of nuclear weapons. Even the Soviets, who probably had less faith in the likely results of disarmament efforts in the 1950s than many in the U.S. government, not only took part in negotiations but offered apparently serious proposals to limit both nuclear and conventional armaments.

The history of the Cold War, especially its first decade, is a study in contrasts: high-blown rhetoric proposing to rid the world of nuclear weapons combined with U.S. and Soviet military programs that equipped both countries with the means to devastate one another's societies. Calls for summit conferences to resolve superpower political conflicts alternated with eyeball-to-eyeball confrontations between East and West, convincing many that a third world war was not only inevitable, but just around the corner. It was a time marked by extraordinary tension that was to last for the better part of two decades.

In trying to understand this unique period, it is important to remember that while hindsight is always 20-20, policymakers must deal with events as they unfold. Situations without precedent are particularly grueling, as the past provides a poor guide to the future. Emerging as allies and joint victors from the most violent war in human history, U.S. and Soviet leaders soon found themselves at odds over a host of issues, some of which, such as how to govern postwar Germany, had seemed manageable as long as the fighting raged. Locked in a confrontation that neither had fully anticipated and for which neither was fully prepared, the differences that had for the most part remained submerged during the war quickly resurfaced and grew more intense. This in turn activated new conflicts, as each side assumed the worst about the intentions of its opponent. As alliance gave way to acrimony, Washington and Moscow sought security in the build-up of their respective military capabilities and, with less focus and determination, in efforts at disarmament. The failure of the latter compelled greater reliance on the former and the predictable consequence was a deepening of hostility and the beginning of the nuclear arms race.

The Origins of the Cold War

The roots of the Cold War can be traced to the winter months of 1942-43 in the Soviet city of Stalingrad. There, on the western banks of the Volga River, in one of the most violent and hard-fought campaigns of the Second World War, the Soviet Army engaged and ultimately defeated Hitler's Wehrmacht. The deep German advance into Soviet territory, under way since June 1941, was finally halted. For the Germans, it was a strategic defeat from which they never recovered. It was also the turning point of the war. Although more than two years of bitter fighting lay ahead in Europe, the German defeat at Stalingrad marked the beginning of the end for the Third Reich.

With increasing confidence in their ultimate victory, the Allies began to consider the shape of the postwar world. Most of the planning fell to the Big Three—President Franklin Roosevelt, Prime Minister Winston Churchill, and Generalissimo Josef Stalin. With the approach of victory, the leaders of the United States, the British Empire, and the Soviet Union found themselves increasingly at odds over a number of important political issues. Two problems proved especially difficult: what to do about Germany after the war and the nature of the political and territorial settlement in Eastern Europe. The Big Three met twice—in November 1943 in Tehran and in February 1945 at Yalta—in an effort to iron out their differences. These meetings, despite the resolution of certain problems, did not end the disagreements. If anything, the conflicts deepened and intensified as the Germans went down to defeat.

The Allies had formulated only general guidelines for the postwar occupation and administration of Germany. As a consequence, when the Germans surrendered in May 1945, no one was quite certain what to do. U.S. policy seemed particularly confused. Within the Roosevelt adminstration, some sentiment had existed for a program to occupy and deindustrialize the country, to be followed by its political dismemberment; instead of one Germany there might be a number of small, demilitarized political units of limited sovereignty, at all times under the watchful gaze of the victorious powers. A second option called for retaining a unified if territorially reduced German state that would be stripped of its military power but left to rebuild economically. This too was assumed to require a period of Allied occupation. There were other ideas, all incorporating various aspects of these two plans. At the time of Roosevelt's death in April 1945, however, important ambiguities remained and America's German policy lacked coherence.[1]

Soviet aims were less confused. One of Stalin's central objectives was to utilize what remained of the German industrial base to rebuild the shattered Soviet economy. Roughly half of the U.S.S.R.'s productive capacities had been destroyed in the course of the war and German assets could be of significant value in facilitating the task of reconstruction. In addition, the Soviets were determined to obtain territorial compensation at German and Polish expense; one area in question was a large chunk of Polish real estate along the western border of the Soviet Union that contained more ethnic Russians than Poles. Stalin proposed, with the two Western allies agreeing in principle, that in exchange for this "adjustment," Poland be awarded German territory, specifically those areas of the former Reich that

Churchill, Roosevelt, and Stalin met in February 1945 in the Soviet city of Yalta to finalize plans for the defeat of Nazi Germany and to discuss the future of postwar Europe.

fell to the east of the Oder and Neisse Rivers. Poland would also receive a portion of East Prussia, the remainder going to the U.S.S.R. Finally, Stalin seemed to prefer that what remained of Germany after these territorial adjustments be divided into zones of military occupation, but that the country be treated as a single political and economic entity, thoroughly purged of Nazi influences and bereft of effective military capabilities.

The British, always more suspicious than the Americans of Soviet intentions, feared a Bolshevized Germany in the heart of Europe. They therefore favored the maintenance of a politically and economically unified state, organized along Western democratic lines. They did not oppose, in principle, either the proposed occupation regime or the redrawing of German borders, although they regarded Soviet ambitions in this regard as excessive.

These differences over how to resolve the German Problem immobilized the Allies. As a result, each of the victorious powers (including France) simply administered on an individual basis that part of Germany previously designated as its zone of occupation. The Soviets ran the eastern third of the country, while the United States, Britain, and France divided the western two-thirds. The Allies did establish a control council, nominally vested with administrative responsibility for the whole of Germany, but its mandate, though broad on paper, was never very extensive in practice.

Reparations emerged as a particularly divisive issue. Originally, the Kremlin pressed for the equivalent of $20 billion in reparations, to be satisfied in the form of existing German capital stock, half of which would go to the Soviet Union. In other words, Moscow proposed to its allies that Germany bear at least some of the cost for the reconstruction of Soviet industry by sanctioning the relocation of German industry. The majority of the equipment would be seized in the territory under Soviet control, but the remainder would have to come from the three Western occupation zones. The Kremlin later scaled back its demands but the Western allies remained cool to the Soviet plan. In May 1946, the United States, followed by Britain and France, suspended the transfer of German industrial facilities from west to east. Further complicating relations, the Soviets began to treat the territorial adjustments in Central and Eastern Europe as *faits accomplis*, much to the annoyance of Western officials, who argued that the settlement had to await the conclusion of a proper peace treaty with the successor German state.

For their part, the Soviets complained that the Western countries were proceeding in a laggardly and haphazard fashion to de-Nazify German political life within the areas under their administration—the implication being that their allies were less concerned with doing away with the remnants of National Socialism than with bolstering the positions of conservative, pro-Western German political figures, whatever their past association with Hitler and his party. The War Crimes trials in Nuremberg did little to assuage Soviet sensitivities on this question.

In Eastern Europe, the issues were also territorial and political. Of the several problems in that region, however, it was Poland that proved the least tractable. In addition to the border problems referred to earlier, the Allies disagreed over the composition of the postwar Polish government. When the Germans and the Soviets partitioned Poland in 1939, many of the most prominent Polish leaders fled to Great Britain, where they constituted a government-in-exile. Given the Kremlin's complicity in Poland's disappearance as a sovereign state, these officials were only slightly less hostile to the Soviet Union than they were to Nazis. The feeling was mutual. As Soviet armed forces returned to Poland in 1944, Stalin authorized the creation of a rival group of Polish leaders, known formally as the Committee of National Liberation but soon dubbed the "Lublin Poles" (for the city in Poland that served as their headquarters). It was to this group that the Soviet dictator looked as the nucleus for a postwar provisional government.

The Polish government-in-exile regarded the Lublin Poles as politically illegitimate and little more than Soviet lackeys. The Soviet-supported Poles viewed their counterparts in London as bourgeois reactionaries who had sat out the war in the relative comfort and safety of the British countryside. Churchill did his best to defend the interests of the London Poles, although the military realities on the ground in Poland gave Stalin the upper hand. As the war drew to a close, Roosevelt took it upon himself to mediate, hoping to negotiate a compromise between the two Polish factions and between Stalin and Churchill.

When the Big Three gathered at Yalta in early 1945, the Lublin Poles had already established themselves as the Provisional Na-

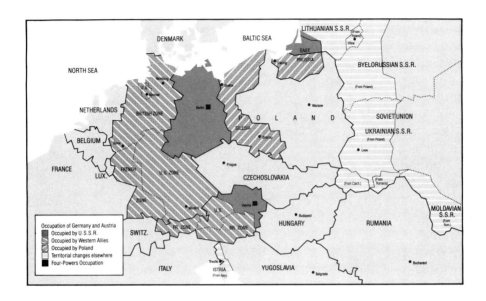

tional Government. Roosevelt and Churchill did succeed, however, in extracting a promise from Stalin to reorganize the new Polish regime on a broader democratic basis and to hold elections as soon after the war as possible. Elections were eventually held, but only "progressive" and "anti-fascist" candidates were allowed to seek office. The London Poles and their supporters were all but frozen out of the process. While the fiction of democratic elections was maintained, the reality fell far short of what American and, to a lesser extent, British policymakers had in mind. Poland became a People's Republic.

Poland was only one of several problems in Eastern Europe that negatively affected postwar relations among the Allies. Soviet-style and Soviet-backed provisional governments were established in Bulgaria and Rumania even before the end of the war in Europe. Regimes friendly to Moscow soon appeared in Czechoslovakia and Hungary. Also in 1945, Yugoslavia and Albania joined the growing list of Soviet-supported "socialist" countries. Closer to home, the Kremlin annexed several thousand square miles of Czechoslovakia and a large piece of Rumania (in addition to having helped itself in 1940 to the three Baltic republics of Estonia, Latvia, and Lithuania). Policymakers in the West became alarmed by this turn of events. To many it seemed that the defeat of one form of totalitarianism had simply facilitated the triumph of another. Within several months of the German defeat, the Grand Alliance was already giving way to mutual hostility and recrimination.

In July 1945, Stalin, Churchill, and Harry Truman (in office only three months) met in the Berlin suburb of Potsdam in an effort to coordinate their European policies and to discuss plans for the final phase of the war against Japan. Although Germany and the situation in Eastern Europe figured prominently on the agenda, agreement on a common strategy for postwar Europe was not forthcoming. It was also at Potsdam that Truman first learned of the successful U.S. atomic bomb test of July 16. After sharing the news with Churchill in private (British scientists had been involved in the program from the outset), Truman told Stalin that the United States had recently detonated a new weapon "of unusual destructive force." Stalin is reported to have responded without emotion, saying only that he hoped the weapon would be used to good effect to hasten Japan's surrender.[2]

Containment and Consolidation

East-West relations deteriorated further in 1946 and early 1947. Especially alarming to the United States was the rise of the French and Italian Communist Parties. In France, the Communists formed part of the first postwar coalition government of the new Fourth Republic led by General Charles de Gaulle; in Italy, the Communist Party was the largest and best organized of the several anti-fascist groups then functioning, and U.S. policymakers feared their coming to power either through the ballot box or a coup d'etat. In southern Europe, a powerful Communist-led insurgency was threatening to topple the Greek government. At the same time, Moscow was pressuring Turkey to accept certain territorial "revisions" disadvantageous to the latter. With Eastern Europe falling behind what Winston Churchill labeled an "Iron Curtain" in a March 1946 speech in Fulton, Missouri, and with the division of Germany looking less and less temporary, U.S. government officials perceived themselves to be in the midst of an ever-widening arc of crisis.

Matters came to a head in February 1947, when the British informed the United States that they were no longer in a financial position to offer meaningful military and economic assistance to the

Greek and Turkish governments. Without American help, the regime in Athens could fall, paving the way for a Communist victory, and the Turks could succumb to Soviet pressure tactics. While the British announcement did not catch Washington by surprise, the administration resolved to act quickly, believing that time was of the essence. On March 12 Truman asked Congress to provide an emergency aid package of $400 million for Greece and Turkey, most of which would be used for military purposes. In requesting the assistance, Truman cast the struggle in terms—totalitarianism versus Western-style democracy—destined to become a hallmark of postwar American foreign policy, arguing that it must be U.S. policy to "support free peoples who are resisting attempted subjugation by armed minorities or by outside pressures." Congress approved the appropriation in May.

In June 1947, Secretary of State George Marshall, in a commencement address at Harvard University, unveiled the U.S. program to assist in the task of reconstructing Europe's war-torn economies. The Marshall Plan, as it became known, made available to participating countries a combination of credits, grants, and loans to rebuild national industries and restore essential services. Between 1948 and 1950, almost $11 billion in U.S. capital flowed to Western Europe via this plan. Beyond whatever element of altruism may have inspired the program, the Marshall Plan made good political and business sense for the United States. An economically revitalized France and Italy were less likely, by American calculation, to embrace Communism than if conditions in these countries were left to deteriorate. In addition, as a country with a large stake in trade, world markets, and overseas investment, the United States had a strong interest in promoting healthy capitalist economies around the globe.

The Soviet Union refused to take part in the Marshall Plan, which it characterized as an American ploy to seize control of Europe's economies. Under Soviet pressure, the Eastern European countries also abstained, although Czechoslovakia had initially communicated some interest in participating. Doubtless, Moscow's decision to stand aside and its insistence that its clients do the same hampered the region's recovery. It was all the Soviets could do to rebuild their own economy in the first few years after the war; extensive assistance to the Eastern Europeans was out of the question.

Not only was the simple crush of events during the first half of 1947 a trying experience for American political authorities, it also did much to focus the ongoing debate over the content and direction of U.S. policy toward the Soviet Union. From May 1945 to the winter of 1947, policymakers in Washington, while acutely sensitive to the steady deterioration of relations with Moscow, resisted the adoption of a strategy built explicitly around the notion of confrontation with the Soviet Union. It was not just the memory of the wartime collaboration with the Kremlin that left U.S. officials reluctant to embark on this course. Neither was it simply the sense that the American people might not support a foreign policy that featured permanent hostility toward another country as its defining characteristic, although that was an important consideration.

Rather, much of the resistance sprang from a sense of confusion concerning the precise nature of the perceived challenge. Were we confronting the Soviet Union as a country or Communism as an ideology? Could they be distinguished? Were Soviet power and ambition the threat to American interests or was it the spread of Communism more generally, which might or might not have much to do with the Kremlin? What would be the political and military implications if we were to seek to separate the two? If they could not be separated? While we had reason to believe that our power was sufficient to deter direct Soviet aggression in Europe and maybe Asia, were we strong enough and rich enough to resist the growth of Communist influence everywhere in the world?

George Kennan, one of the most influential architects of postwar U.S. foreign policy, attempted to answer some of these questions in two documents: the so-called "Long Telegram," written in Moscow in February 1946 while he was U.S. chargé d'affaires, and "The Sources of Soviet Conduct," an article carried by the influential journal *Foreign Affairs* in July 1947. The thrust of Kennan's argument was that a policy of patient firmness and of force adroitly and judiciously applied could contain the Soviet Union's imperial appetite at an acceptable cost to the United States. He was careful to point out that, while a serious challenge to American interests, the Kremlin was unlikely to provoke a military confrontation with Washington, given the disparities in power and the traditional Russian aversion to risk. He foresaw a long struggle between the United States and the Soviet Union but one that need not result in war. He also seemed to distinguish between the threat posed to this country and its allies by the U.S.S.R. and the more general problem of revolutionary turmoil and indigenous Communist insurgencies.[3]

Many, including President Truman, adopted Kennan's rhetoric while seeming to overlook or ignore much of his argument and many of his specific recommendations. For example, when it came time to provide the public rationale for the containment policy, the Truman administration tended to describe the threat as global in its dimensions, painting a picture of a worldwide contest between the forces of "freedom" on the one hand, and "slavery" on the other. Containment soon came to mean a kind of generalized resistance to Communism in all its forms rather than opposition to the further territorial and/or political aggrandizement of the Soviet Union. Kennan spent much of the next 30 years distinguishing what he meant by containment from what the concept would come to represent to successive U.S. administrations.

In practice, U.S. policy was much less ambitious than the rhetoric implied. By 1947, the United States had undertaken only two major political initiatives in Europe, one to prop up the Greek and Turkish governments and a second to help in the economic reconstruction of the United Kingdom, France, Italy, and the Benelux countries. Moreover, at this point the United States did not possess the military forces to act as the Western world's gendarme; not only was its stockpile of atomic weapons relatively small (about a dozen weapons in all), but its conventional forces had been reduced dramatically since the conclusion of the war: from a high of 12 million in the summer of 1945, U.S. armed forces had declined to 1.6 million by July 1947. While obviously alarmed by recent developments in international politics, neither the budget-balancing Democratic administration nor the tight-fisted Republican Congress were as yet prepared to undertake a comprehensive military build-up.

The evolution of Soviet policy between the end of the war and the first part of 1947 is more difficult to analyze, in large part because it took place in secrecy. Stalin, after all, chose not to write his memoirs and even if he had we might find them less than useful for our purposes. In retrospect, however, it appears that the Soviet leadership may have been almost as surprised by the sudden downturn in Allied relations following the war as their counterparts in Washington and London. Doubtless, Stalin anticipated a negative if not a hostile reaction to his forced communization of Eastern Europe, but he may have believed that the West's indignation was largely for public consumption. In Stalin's mind, the prerogatives of power might well have suggested no other outcome. What else do great powers do when they have won a costly and protracted war but redraw the map to their advantage? Given a choice between maintaining at least correct relations with Washington and consolidating Soviet power in Central and Eastern Europe, we can assume that Stalin hesitated hardly at all.

Regarding conditions in Western and Southern Europe, the Soviets may have calculated that if the economic turmoil produced Communist or Communist-leaning governments, all to the good, as long as the results could be realized at essentially no cost to the U.S.S.R. They also may have thought that the United States could not possibly assign them responsibility for events hundreds of miles from their borders and beyond the effective reach of Soviet armed forces. In 1947, they were hardly in a position to lend the French, Italian, and Greek Communists much in the way of direct material assistance in any event, whatever they may have wanted to do.

The "German Question" was more of a problem. Stalin probably preferred a temporary occupation, followed by a territorial settlement and the establishment of a leftist-oriented regime. Germany might then become a political buffer zone between East and West, posing no threat to Soviet security. Finland may be the closest analogue. Such was not to be the case, however, as efforts to forge a unified, neutral, demilitarized, and reduced Germany foundered. The West must be held partially responsible for this turn of events, as its clear preference was to accept the division of Germany, if this was the price for keeping the western two-thirds of the country in friendly hands. In response, the Soviet Union tightened its grip within its own zone of occupation.

Looking back on the period, it is evident that the overriding Soviet preoccupation was the consolidation of its position in Eastern Europe and not, as it appeared to some Western observers, the further extension of its empire. While it is true that Communist or Communist-leaning regimes were soon established in most of the countries occupied by Soviet armed forces in the immediate postwar years, it can also be argued that the Kremlin evidenced no great appetite for additional conquests in areas beyond the control of its military. Western efforts to discern the Kremlin's motives at the time were complicated by the tone of Soviet rhetoric toward its erstwhile allies, a tone both militant and confrontational. Stalin's famous "two-camp" speech of February 1946, for example, in which he refused to rule out the possibility of a new world war (brought on by "contradictions" among capitalist countries), did much to promote the sense of acute crisis that gripped many Western capitals during this period.

Part of the Soviet Union's reluctance to press for even greater territorial and political gains stemmed from the expressed opposition of the United States. In 1946, for example, Soviet forces withdrew from the northern part of Iran under American pressure, rather than risk a confrontation with Washington. The United States also rebuffed a Soviet proposal that the U.S.S.R. be awarded an occupation zone in Japan in return for its contribution to the latter's defeat. The Soviets, however, could have demanded the imposition of a Communist government in Finland in 1945; they certainly had the physical power to establish one at the time. That they didn't suggests a preoccupation with digesting what they had already attained. Beyond the dangers that might have attended a more ambitious Soviet policy, any effort to extend Moscow's territorial dominion also would have been costly in economic terms. Whatever combination of factors may have influenced Stalin's thinking, Soviet forces stayed put at war's end.

From the Berlin Blockade to the War in Korea

In 1948, U.S.-Soviet relations went from bad to worse. Early in the year, a Soviet-supported political faction engineered the overthrow of the left-leaning coalition government in Czechoslovakia. With the success of that operation, the last vestige of Western-style democracy in Eastern Europe disappeared. In June, Stalin imposed his famous blockade of West Berlin. The Soviet leader's motives remain obscure although they appear to have had something to do with placing pressure on the West to halt—or at least reopen for negotiation—the economic and political integration of the American, British, and French occupation zones in Germany then under way. The Western allies, however, saw the Soviet action as an effort to force them out of Berlin and as a possible prelude to a new European war.

In response, they undertook to resupply the former German capital by air, thus reaffirming both their right to be in Berlin (under the terms of a September 1944 agreement signed by representatives of the United States, Great Britain, and the Soviet Union and confirmed by the Big Three five months later at Yalta) and their determination not to be evicted by force. The airlift was successful on both counts. The blockade must be considered a failure from the Soviet perspec-

tive, as it did not compel the West to reconsider its German policy; on the contrary, the process of West German integration continued apace. The blockade ended in May 1949. In September, the Federal Republic of Germany officially came into being and the following month Moscow sanctioned the establishment of the German Democratic Republic (comprised of the Soviet occupation zone), thus cementing the political division of the former Reich.

Three other events in 1949—the signing of the North Atlantic Treaty in April, the detonation of the first Soviet atomic bomb in August, and the victory of Mao Tse-tung in China in October— intensified the division between East and West. The first two events imparted a manifestly military character to the competition. The third rendered it global.

The significance of NATO, as the North Atlantic alliance came to be known, was twofold. First, it marked the end of the vacillation in Western policy toward the Soviet Union. NATO was and remains a formal political and military alliance directed against the U.S.S.R. and its Eastern European allies. As such, it constituted an explicit symbol of Europe's bipolarity, or the division of the continent into rival blocs. It also provided a legal and structural basis for that cleavage. Second, and equally important, it was the mechanism by which the United States officially coupled its security to that of Western Europe.

It was an unprecedented step for Washington. Never before had any American administration pledged in advance to regard an attack against another country or group of countries outside the Western Hemisphere as an attack against the vital interests of the United States. Moreover, NATO obligated the United States to come to the military assistance of its new allies in the event of a future war in Europe, subject to the provision that such action be taken in accordance with established constitutional procedures (i.e., that only Congress could actually declare war). U.S. adherence to the North Atlantic Treaty, while generally popular, was not without its opponents. Republican Senator Robert Taft of Ohio warned against such an open-ended commitment, but in the end the Truman administration prevailed. The Senate advised ratification in July 1949, by a vote of 82 to 13.[4]

The Soviet nuclear test and the "fall" of China were in some sense more important to the evolution of America's Soviet policy than the creation of NATO. Both were instrumental in provoking a far-reaching reexamination of the goals of U.S. defense strategy and the means by which it could be implemented. Early in 1950, a combined group of State and Defense Department officials, under the direction of Paul N. Nitze, took the lead in exploring the implications for U.S. security of a nuclear-armed Soviet Union. The result was the National Security Council document, NSC-68. The report was presented to President Truman for his consideration in April of that year.

The authors of NSC-68 argued that the Soviet threat to American and Western interests would increase markedly over the course of the next five years; while attaching a low probability to an intentional Soviet military attack against the West, they cautioned that such a development could not be ruled out. The document drew special attention to the likely growth of the Kremlin's nuclear weapons stockpile, which could reach a total of 200 bombs by mid-1954—more than enough, it was argued, to lay waste to much of Western Europe and to many vital centers in the United States.

Among its many recommendations, the report urged a dramatic increase in U.S. defense spending between 1950 and 1954, arguing that such an effort could be undertaken without a reduction in the U.S. standard of living. Informal estimates of what might be required to implement the document's recommendations ranged as high as $40 billion per year, or roughly three and a half times the $13.5 billion ceiling on defense spending that Truman had established the year before.[5] The report also pressed for an expanded army and air force. It went on to note that if its recommendations for increasing U.S. military power were adopted, "the United States would have the capability of eliminating the disparity between its military strength and the exigencies of the situation we face; eventually of gaining the initiative in the 'cold' war and of materially delaying if not stopping the Soviet offensives in war itself."[6]

The tone of NSC-68 was one of urgency: that since the discovery the previous September of the Soviet atomic bomb test, the dangers to Western security had expanded enormously and that only a concerted program to rebuild U.S. defenses could reliably deter a new world war. The document aroused considerable controversy within the government. Many, including George Kennan, thought it overly dramatic in its portrayal of the Soviet threat, paying insufficient attention to the Kremlin's economic and military weaknesses and its aversion to risk-taking in foreign policy. NSC-68 was also criticized for its failure to distinguish adequately between the challenges posed by the Soviet Union, on the one hand, and international Communism, on the other. Lastly, critics charged that insufficient consideration had been given to the economic costs of a comprehensive program to rearm the United States. If the estimate of the threat was exaggerated, the country could end up spending billions of unnecessary dollars on defense—dollars that could be better directed to other purposes.

North Korea's attack against its southern neighbor on June 25, 1950, cut short the debate over NSC-68. To the extent that they encouraged the North Korean aggression, the Soviets could not have devised a better strategy to guarantee Truman's adoption of the Nitze plan had they consciously set out to do so. Here, it seemed, was graphic proof of the report's central contention: That the Soviet Union, with the active assistance of its Communist clients, would exploit perceived Western vulnerabilities at every available opportunity, even at the risk of war. Some within the administration drew an even more alarming conclusion. In their view, the Korean war might be a tactical diversion, to be followed by a general Soviet military offensive against Western Europe.

The actual course of the conflict in Korea—the initial success of the North Korean offensive, the American and United Nations counterattack, the subsequent retreat of Communist forces to the Chinese border, China's military intervention, and the eventual stalemate not far from the original dividing line between North and South—is less important for our purposes than what the war revealed about the character of the international system and its evolution since the Second World War.

The war in Korea was the first and to date the only direct and prolonged military struggle between East and West. It was the only occasion in which the United States, at the head of a broad coalition of non-Communist countries, engaged the armed forces of the "socialist commonwealth"—even though the only two Communist nations to supply troops were China and North Korea, the Soviets having decided to assume a less conspicuous role. It is significant in this context that neither the United States nor the Soviet Union resorted to the use of nuclear weapons (although in 1953 the Eisenhower administration communicated through diplomatic channels that it would not rule out that option) and that the war ended in a draw. What this suggests is the realization on both sides that to employ nuclear weapons in the service of limited military objectives would involve risks disproportionate to the provocation. That the United States should have reached this conclusion is especially revealing, as the crisis came at a time of overwhelming American nuclear superiority; had Washington chosen to widen the war by attacking Chinese territory with nuclear weapons, Beijing would have been powerless to respond in kind. What may have deterred U.S. policymakers—beyond the expressed opposition of many of the governments fighting alongside the United States in Korea—was fear of a Soviet counterattack against NATO Europe, possibly provoking a third world war.

Starting Over: Eisenhower's Election and the Death of Stalin

The conflict in Korea had dragged on for two and a half years when Dwight D. Eisenhower defeated his Democratic challenger, Adlai Stevenson, for the presidency. Eisenhower owed his victory, at least in part, to the public's dissatisfaction with the Truman administration's foreign and military policies. The American people held the former president and his advisers responsible for both the Communist takeover in China and what was commonly regarded as a debacle in Korea. Eisenhower and the Republicans came to power promising to end the Korean War. They also stressed the need to move beyond the mere "containment" of international Communism and to "roll back" its various ill-gotten gains.

Much of the Republican case against the Truman administration was politically motivated, having little to do with reality. The Democrats no more lost China, for example, than Herbert Hoover caused the Great Depression. The United States was at most a minor actor in the 20-year struggle between General Chiang Kai-shek and his Kuomintang forces and the Chinese Communists, led by Mao Tse-tung. To hold the Democrats responsible for the defeat of the former was preposterous. On the war in Korea, Republican arguments were equally self-serving. Not only was the Truman administration blamed for the outbreak of the conflict, it was also criticized for its failure to prosecute the war with sufficient vigor and determination—implying that a Republican president would have "fought on to victory."

Lost in the noise of the 1952 presidential campaign was the reality that the United States had settled, in fact, on a very clear strategy for managing the Soviet "threat" over the long term. Although it would undergo constant revision and fine-tuning during the next decade and a half, containment—with its emphasis on restraining

Soviet conduct and deterring Communist aggression through the maintenance of American military superiority—would remain the bedrock of U.S. policy. While the Truman administration embraced the strategy incrementally and only after a prolonged internal debate, by 1950 the policy was firmly in place, perhaps best symbolized by the president's endorsement of NSC-68 in the fall of that year. Until the advent of the Nixon administration in 1969, containment was to have no rival. To this day, American foreign policy remains loyal to many of its precepts, notwithstanding the many and vast changes that have taken place in international politics since its first appearance.

Continuities aside, 1953 was an important year in U.S.-Soviet relations. In October, President Eisenhower authorized a "New Look" in U.S. defense policy, which was in actuality a retreat from the program developed at considerable length in NSC-68. At the heart of that document had been a proposal to equip the United States with military forces, both nuclear and conventional, adequate to defeat the Soviet Union in the event of war. While a portion of that burden would be shouldered by America's allies, the United States would assume most of the responsibility. The Eisenhower administration rejected that plan in favor of a more modest program, centered on the expansion of strategic air power and a parallel increase in the size of the nuclear weapons stockpile. Appropriations for the army, navy, and air force were to be reduced, at least initially.[7]

The logic was more economic than military. Eisenhower strongly believed that the most effective way to maintain American strength was through an expansion of the industrial base; a significantly enlarged defense budget, in his view, would require the imposition of new taxes and divert resources from the civilian economy. The president's decision placed him at odds with many of his own advisers, who had looked forward to a more assertive U.S. foreign policy, backed by a resurgent military establishment. The New Look immediately cast doubt on the determination as well as the ability of the new administration to make good on its campaign rhetoric.

Something had to give. In line with Eisenhower's preferences, U.S. defense spending decreased in fiscal 1955 (the first year for which the Republican administration was fully responsible) by some 15 percent from the year before. It increased a scant two-tenths of 1 percent in fiscal 1956. Of the four military services, only the air force escaped major budgetary reductions. In keeping with Eisenhower's fiscal austerity, the administration early on put forward a new political-military strategy for dealing with the twin challenges of Soviet power and international Communism. Henceforth, Secretary of State John Foster Dulles announced in January 1954, the United States would rely on its "massive retaliatory power," by which he meant mostly the Strategic Air Command, to safeguard Western security. The way to deter aggression, Dulles argued, was "to depend primarily upon a great capacity to retaliate instantly by means and at places of our choosing." The Secretary of State went on to note:

> Now the Department of Defense and the Joint Chiefs
> of Staff can shape our military establishment to fit what
> is our policy instead of having to try to be ready to
> meet the enemy's many choices. And that permits of
> a selection of military means instead of a multiplication
> of means. And as a result it is now possible to get, and
> to share, more security at less cost.[8]

Missing from the initial Dulles rendering of "massive retaliation" was any clear sense of proportion or scale. Would an East German military foray into West German territory result in a full nuclear strike against the Soviet Union and its satellites? What was the threshold for U.S. action? Moreover, how credible was it for Washington to threaten Moscow with atomic devastation if, as reported, the Soviet Union could deliver nuclear weapons to American soil in response? Was it wise to concentrate so much U.S. military power in a single branch of the armed forces? What if the need for large-scale conventional military forces were to arise?

Dulles went to considerable lengths in the months following his articulation of the new U.S. strategy to clarify, amend, and expand on its meaning. American nuclear power would only be used in defense of the West's most vital interests. The United States would continue, of course, to consult with its allies whenever circumstances warranted. No, the army and navy would not be left to atrophy.

Qualifications notwithstanding, massive retaliation was an important departure in U.S. strategy. While retaining the essentially defensive character of containment, it sought to implement that policy through different—and less expensive—means. The most noteworthy effect of the Republican departure from the Truman line was to increase dramatically U.S. reliance on nuclear weapons to safeguard Western security. It also placed enormous pressure on the administration to stand up to any future Russian military moves beyond, if not within, the Soviet sphere of influence, owing to this country's "massive" nuclear superiority.

In the Soviet Union even greater changes were under way. On March 5, 1953, Josef Stalin died. A power struggle ensued that pitted Stalin's heir apparent, Georgi Malenkov, against Nikita Khrushchev, whom the Soviet dictator had brought to Moscow some years before to help manage Party affairs at the national level. Malenkov became head of the government while Khrushchev consolidated his position within the Party apparatus. An uneasy duumvirate emerged that left Western observers uncertain as to who was really in charge. The Kremlin didn't help matters much by insisting that the power-sharing arrangement was the natural order of things, glossing over the fact that for twenty-five years Stalin had ruled the Soviet Union as a latter-day Tsar. They called the new system "collective leadership." It wasn't long, however, before the Malenkov-Khrushchev rivalry broke into the open.

For the moment, it was business as usual. The American and Soviet governments continued to cast a wary eye on each other, much as they had throughout the entire postwar period. Stalin's death led to no radical departures in Soviet policy in 1953, either domestically or internationally, and the Eisenhower administration anticipated no great transformation in the superpower relationship.

The First "Spirit of Geneva"

One of the first clear signs to the West that something was afoot occurred in March 1954, when Malenkov delivered a speech that cast doubt on the ability of the "socialist community" to prevail over the imperialists in the event of a new world war.[9] The Soviet premier warned explicitly that a global military engagement featuring the widespread use of nuclear weapons could spell the end of world civilization. This pessimistic assessment placed Malenkov at odds with the conventional Soviet view that while a third world war would be enormously destructive, Communism would emerge victorious. Significantly, the Malenkov thesis was not echoed by other members of the leadership. More to the point, Khrushchev denounced it as contrary to the laws of Marxism-Leninism and a manifestation of bourgeois thinking at its worst. For this and a host of other sins that Khrushchev was only too happy to detail, Malenkov was forced to resign from the leadership in February 1955. Khrushchev became the undisputed first among equals within the Kremlin.

Having destroyed Malenkov politically, Khrushchev proceeded to adopt much of the former's foreign policy line, including the notion of a limited detente with the United States. The Soviet call for a thaw in the Cold War made sense from Khrushchev's perspective. The activist rhetoric of the Eisenhower administration, coupled with American military superiority, must have alarmed the Kremlin leadership. Who could say what might provoke the United States to unleash its power against the U.S.S.R.? Might not Washington try to make good on its commitment to assist in the "liberation" of the "captive nations" of Eastern Europe, given half a chance? What about Communist China, a Soviet ally? How safe was Mao Tse-tung from American fury? A partial relaxation in tensions was one means of coping with what Khrushchev must have seen as a particularly dangerous phase in relations between Moscow and Washington.

The principal beneficiary of the thaw in U.S.-Soviet relations was Austria. Divided after the war into four occupation zones, the Austrians had yet to recover their independence. For ten years, the former World War II allies had argued over how to restore the country's independence and when to withdraw their forces. Quite unexpectedly, from the Western perspective, the pace of negotiations quickened early in 1955. Eventually, the occupying powers struck a deal. Austria's sovereignty would be restored on two conditions: that it be politically neutral and that it have essentially no military establishment. The West jumped at the offer and the Austrian State Treaty was signed in May 1955.

The Kremlin may have hoped that the Austrian solution would serve as a model for a German settlement. If so, their hopes were misplaced. The reintegration of West Germany into the Western community had proceeded too far. Over strong Soviet protest, the Federal Republic joined NATO ten days before the signing of the treaty restoring Austria's independence. In response, the Soviet Union induced the German Democratic Republic, Poland, Czechoslovakia, Hungary, Bulgaria, Rumania, and Albania to supplement their bilateral military ties to Moscow with a multilateral alliance, known formally as the Warsaw Treaty Organization. Europe's bipolarization was now complete.

Despite this and other setbacks in 1954 and 1955, the first postwar detente between East and West continued to gather momentum, culminating in a July 1955 summit conference in Geneva. In attendance were Eisenhower, Khrushchev, nominal Soviet Premier Nikolai Bulganin, British Prime Minister Anthony Eden, and French leader Edgar Faure. The conference accomplished very little. Although discussed, the German problem was not resolved, nor could the heads of government reconcile the different Soviet and Western proposals for general and complete disarmament. No surprises there. Eisenhower did suggest that the two sides permit aerial reconnaissance of each other's national territory to reduce the risk of war (the so-called "Open Skies" proposal), but the Soviets demurred. The president also proposed that the United States and the Soviet Union exchange blueprints of one another's military plants and facilities. Again, Kremlin leaders declined. The conference adjourned with smiles and handshakes but little else. Nothing had really changed. The true significance of Geneva was that it had taken place at all.

Meanwhile, the arms race accelerated. By 1955, both superpowers had successfully detonated sophisticated thermonuclear weapons in the multi-megaton range, supplementing their burgeoning arsenals of atomic bombs. Moreover, each was acquiring the means to deliver these powerful new weapons over great distances. In the United States, the medium-range, all-jet B-47 was just entering the inventory, with the much larger and more capable B-52 scheduled to follow in 1956. The Soviets had two long-range bombers in production at the time, either of which could deposit nuclear weapons against targets in the American homeland. Whatever the marginal improvement in political relations, the military competition was becoming more intense and moving onto new and unexplored terrain.

The Wall, Berlin / *Ronald Searle, 1963*

4 | False Starts and New Dangers 1956–1968

Between 1945 and 1955, relations between the superpowers could not have been much worse, short of war. Crisis succeeded crisis as the United States and the Soviet Union squared off in a kind of global chess match, the military power of each rapidly overshadowing that of every other country. During that first Cold War decade—from the Nazi surrender to the Geneva summit—each side also sought to enhance its influence by acquiring allies, clients, and dependents from one end of the world to the other, often formalizing these arrangements through treaties and less formal agreements.

By the middle of the 1950s, much of the world had been drawn into these two rival camps, led by Washington and Moscow, respectively. Such a process did not come about spontaneously. Nor did it occur without generating considerable tension, hostility, and fear. The sense of unremitting crisis in international relations during the first ten years after the war was a direct and predictable outgrowth of this far-reaching political realignment. There was, after all, no blueprint for assuming the mantle of a superpower.

By 1955, the Cold War had assumed a certain structural dimension. In the parts of the world that mattered most to the superpowers, the dividing line between East and West was for the most part unambiguous. To anchor this division, the two sides sought to impose a kind of quasi-legitimate order within their respective spheres, both to defend what they saw as "belonging" to them and to ward off unwelcome change. That process was largely complete by the mid-1950s. As long as neither country sought to disturb this status quo by force of arms, there was little reason to expect that an imperfect peace might not endure for the indefinite future. More than any other single development, it was this mutual if implicit acceptance of bipolarity that had made possible the limited detente of 1955.

Not that superpower relations lacked drama after mid-decade. In the thirteen years separating the summit in Geneva from the election of Richard Nixon in 1968, the United States and the Soviet Union found themselves in a number of bone-chilling confrontations. Those over Berlin and Cuba, in particular, were no less intense than the most severe crises of the early postwar period. If bipolarity served to reduce the incidence of superpower crises after 1955, it had little impact on the intensity of those that did develop. Yet beneath the surface, important, if subtle, changes in the relationship—having mostly to do with the character of the strategic military balance—were taking place; these would pave the way for the first and largely unsuccessful efforts by Washington and Moscow to regulate aspects of their political and military competition.

Sputnik, the Missile Gap, and the Beginnings of Arms Control

This second phase of the Cold War began, however, not on a co-operative note but with a crisis. More correctly, it began with two crises that overlapped in time. In late October 1956, the Hungarian people forced the collapse of the Soviet-backed regime in Budapest, making possible the formation of a new government that included elements hostile to the Kremlin. The new leadership soon announced that Hungary would withdraw from the Warsaw Treaty Organization. Following a brief period of vacillation, the Soviets dispatched the Red Army to crush the revolt. Resistance was spirited but short lived. With Moscow's support, an orthodox Communist government was soon installed and thousands of Hungarians who had participated in the revolution fled to the West.

At roughly the same time, the United Kingdom, France, and Israel undertook a military assault against Egypt, ostensibly to reclaim control of the Suez Canal, which Egyptian president Nasser had recently "nationalized." A second purpose of the campaign was to unseat Nasser. The United States pressed its two most important European allies and Israel to abandon the attack. When they resisted,

Washington cut off British and French oil supplies from Latin America and sponsored a United Nations General Assembly resolution calling for an immediate cease-fire. Reluctantly, London and Paris ordered a halt to their military operations. The Israelis had no choice but to accede to American pressure (although they did manage to capture the Sinai peninsula first). Nasser kept his job and his canal.

In retrospect, what is significant about these two crises is what *didn't* happen. The United States, for example, did not send its forces to assist the Hungarian "freedom fighters," despite domestic political pressures to do so. Rather than seize the opportunity to roll back Soviet power in Europe, the Eisenhower administration stood aside, for all intents and purposes content to substitute high-sounding rhetoric for military action. For their part, the Soviets took no direct steps to assist Nasser in his hour of need, other than to propose the sending of a joint U.S.-Soviet military contingent to separate the combatants. They did threaten London and Paris in a kind of vague way, reminding leaders in both capitals that the Kremlin now possessed long-range missiles armed with nuclear weapons, but not until after American opposition was manifest and the Suez operation had begun to unravel.[1]

This is not to suggest that either superpower should have meddled in the dramatic affairs of the opposing bloc. On the contrary, to have done so could have had catastrophic consequences. It is to suggest, however, that had the Hungarian revolution, in particular, occurred eight years before, the outcome might have been different. In 1948, the division of Europe had yet to be finalized and the United States, with its nuclear monopoly, might have been tempted to lend a hand to the revolutionary government in Hungary. By 1956, such a course of action was already out of the question and each superpower had essentially a free hand to manage the situation within its own sphere as it saw fit, with little fear of outside interference.

The second decade of the Cold War had gotten off to a rocky start, at least from the American perspective. The news was to get worse before it got better. In October 1957, the U.S. public was shocked to learn that the Kremlin had lofted into orbit the first man-made satellite, demonstrating that it could produce and launch large, long-range ballistic missiles. If the Russians could place Sputnik in space, couldn't they use the same kind of rocket to deliver nuclear weapons to American cities? The answer from the administration was maybe, but that it didn't matter all that much anyway. What the American people had no way of knowing at the time was that no more than half a dozen of these SS-6 missiles would be deployed over the course of the next five years, and that even if the missiles were to be launched, there was no guarantee that they would arrive on target. Moreover, these few weapons could do precious little to change the strategic military balance between the superpowers, which from 1957 to the mid-1960s would strongly favor the United States.

Eisenhower initially resisted staff recommendations that he sanction increased appropriations for U.S. missile programs. Confident that the American nuclear deterrent was more than adequate and that the three services were already receiving more than enough funds to underwrite their developmental work on land- and sea-based missiles, he saw no compelling reason to supplement their budgets. Secret U-2 overflights of Soviet territory, begun in 1956, confirmed the slow pace of the Kremlin's missile-building program, adding to Eisenhower's disinclination to take dramatic action in response in Sputnik. Eventually, some additional allocations were forthcoming to appease Congress and public opinion. In addition, the president authorized the deployment of a limited number of U.S. medium-range ballistic missiles in Britain, Italy, and Turkey, pending the start-up of full-scale production of the intercontinental-range systems and the introduction of the first ballistic-missile submarines.

Given the generally high state of tension from the latter part of 1956 to the fall of 1957, it is somewhat surprising that the two governments took several important steps in the direction of negotiated arms control beginning in 1958. Prior to this time, the two superpowers had tended to communicate their ideas for the reduction of nuclear and conventional armaments in the form of comprehensive proposals calling for general and complete disarmament. The presentation of these plans—and there were many of them between 1946 and 1957—became increasingly ritualistic as the Cold War dragged on. Each side's proposals, offered with great ceremony, contained elements that the opposing camp could not accept. While the major Western powers and the Soviet Union did negotiate directly during these years in an effort to resolve their differences on the basis of these draft treaties, the results were meager. It is too harsh to characterize these proposals as mere public relations gambits, but it is not inappropriate to question the sincerity with which they were offered.

In 1958, the pattern was broken. Following a high-level exchange of letters, the United States and the Soviet Union agreed to investigate whether and under what conditions they might conclude an agreement to terminate nuclear weapons testing. Beyond the potential value of a comprehensive test ban in slowing the further development of U.S. and Soviet nuclear weapons programs, the decision to pursue negotiations was significant for what it suggested about the readiness of East and West to set aside their proposals for general and complete disarmament and to negotiate in earnest on discrete aspects or dimensions of the arms race.

The meeting that summer of the first "conference of experts," involving American, Soviet, and British specialists on the monitoring of nuclear weapons tests, signaled, therefore, a little-appreciated turning point in postwar diplomacy: the ascendance of arms control over disarmament as the focus of U.S. and Soviet efforts to constrain their military competition. It is difficult to overemphasize the importance of this development. Without such a shift in emphasis, it is doubtful that Washington and Moscow could have made even the limited progress in controlling their nuclear arsenals that they were able to achieve in subsequent decades.[2]

Even though the conference attained only modest success in its deliberations (elaborating many of the requirements for an effective regime to ensure compliance with a test ban), the fact that it had convened at all—and agreed on anything—set it apart from most other superpower security-related conferences of the postwar period. Negotiations for a total ban on nuclear weapons testing, which formally convened in November 1958, continued sporadically throughout the remainder of President Eisenhower's second term, into the Kennedy years, and beyond. A limited ban, prohibiting the testing of nuclear weapons in the atmosphere, underwater, and in space, was signed by American, British, and Soviet representatives in Moscow in August 1963. That treaty remains in force.

Also in November 1958, a group of political and technical experts from NATO and Warsaw Pact countries met to consider the problem of reducing the risks of nuclear surprise attack. The meeting accomplished very little, as the participants couldn't even settle on an agenda and the conference adjourned (never to resume) six weeks later.

The most visible consequence of the apparent superpower interest in arms control was a moratorium on nuclear weapons testing which lasted from November 1958 to September 1961. Under pressure from an aroused international public, deeply concerned over the possible environmental and ecological consequences of continued atmospheric testing, the two superpowers and the United Kingdom agreed to suspend their activities in this area, at least temporarily. The moratorium ended amid great controversy nine months after the inauguration of President John F. Kennedy, as the Soviet Union undertook a new series of tests. The Kremlin justified its decision by arguing that the West had been the first to abandon the informal agreement when the French, who had never agreed to abide by the moratorium to begin with, tested a nuclear weapon in the atmosphere in 1960. In addition, President Eisenhower had stated in late 1960 that the United States would resume its testing program whenever it determined that it was in the national interest to do so. Whatever the precise sequence of events, the moratorium collapsed and a new and particularly active round of above-ground nuclear tests began which continued until the conclusion of the Limited Test Ban Treaty 22 months later.

Corresponding to these ups and downs in arms control, superpower relations during the last two years of the Eisenhower presidency were an odd mixture of acrimony and stillborn efforts at accommodation. The Berlin crisis of 1958, which pitted the Soviet Union and the German Democratic Republic against the three Western allies and the Federal Republic over the status of the former German capital, was followed by an easing of that confrontation and Khrushchev's 1959 visit to the United States. In an attempt to build on the so-called "spirit of Camp David," Eisenhower journeyed to Geneva in 1960 to meet again with his colorful Soviet counterpart in what was to be the second and last of the Big Four summits during his administration—only to have the conference break up over the Kremlin's downing of an American U-2 spy plane caught flying over Soviet territory. There were no serious security-oriented negotiations between the superpowers in the remaining seven months of the Republican administration. On this disappointing and confusing note, Eisenhower's second term drew to a close.

The Kennedy-Johnson Years:
Assured Destruction and Flexible Response

The eight years of the Kennedy and Johnson administrations constitute an especially tumultuous, almost cacophonous period in the relationship between the superpowers. They began with a string of crises that rivaled those of the late 1940s and early 1950s and concluded with an agreement in principle to explore the negotiation of limits on each side's strategic nuclear forces. They witnessed the disintegration of the Sino-Soviet alliance, the withdrawal of France from the military component of NATO, American involvement in and preoccupation with the war in Vietnam, and the Warsaw Pact invasion of Czechoslovakia. Between 1961 and 1968, the American polity went from being one of the most self-confident and self-satisfied in the world to one of the most divided and dispirited. In the Soviet Union, Khrushchev lost his job to a troika of faceless bureaucrats in ill-fitting suits, or so they seemed to most Americans at the time. Much of this history lies beyond the scope of this analysis; what follows, of necessity, is a selective treatment of those issues that bear directly on the subject of this book: the superpowers and nuclear weapons.

When John F. Kennedy took the oath of office on January 20, 1961, the country stood on the threshold of what its people confidently believed would be a decade of unparalleled economic opportunity and continued preeminence in world affairs. The new president's inaugural address, one of the most carefully crafted and evocative speeches of its kind ever delivered, both reassured the American people that such was likely to be their future and challenged them to make it so. In its simple, short phrases can still be found the most expressive articulation of what it meant to be an American sixteen years after the Second World War: to be a citizen of the richest and most powerful industrial democracy in the world that in 1961 was still producing well over a third of the world's manufactured goods.

In that address, Kennedy laid out his vision of American foreign policy, reassuring our allies and warning our adversaries that "we will bear any burden, pay any price, meet any hardship, support any friend, oppose any foe to assure the survival and success of liberty." "This much we pledge," he declared, "and more." Never before had an American president promised so much (and never again would the American people expect him to). We have no reliable record of the Soviet leadership's sentiments concerning Kennedy's address, of course, but Khrushchev and his colleagues must have scratched their heads in wonderment. Could he mean it?

The Kremlin received a partial answer almost immediately when the new administration, making good on a campaign pledge, submitted a request to Congress for supplementary military appropriations, to "rebuild America's defenses"—the Democrats having made the case that they had been permitted to atrophy during the preceding eight years. It was the down payment on what was to become a significant expansion in U.S. military capabilities over the next several years. While general purpose forces received a healthy infusion of additional funds, it was the remarkable growth in American strategic nuclear power between 1961 and 1967 that drew the most attention.

In seven years, the United States built and deployed 1000 intercontinental-range ballistic missiles (ICBMs) and over 30 ballistic missile submarines. The Eisenhower administration had authorized both of these programs but it fell to Kennedy and his advisers to determine the exact level of effort. In each case, the decision was a compromise among competing points of view.[3] From proposals that the United States deploy anywhere between 250 and 10,000 Minuteman ICBMs, the administration settled on the figure of 1000, which, together with anticipated submarine deployments (increased from 26 to 41 under the Democrats) and the 600 B-52 long-range bombers, was considered to constitute an adequate deterrent. That calculation appears to have been fairly arbitrary, as no one knew precisely what it took to deter.

As the new missiles became operational, Secretary of Defense Robert McNamara, his staff, and the uniformed military scrutinized the strategy that would guide their use in the event of war. McNamara himself was simultaneously drawn in two directions. Strongly inclined toward a posture of minimum deterrence—that is, building the smallest number of advanced nuclear weapon systems necessary to dissuade the Soviet Union from striking first with its own forces— McNamara also realized that the United States would soon enjoy an overwhelming numerical advantage over the U.S.S.R. with respect to ICBMs and SLBMs (submarine-launched ballistic missiles). That advantage was likely to be so pronounced as to enable this country to eliminate virtually all of the Kremlin's nuclear arsenal in a preemptive attack, at least for the next several years.

During the first part of the Kennedy administration, therefore, the Defense Secretary championed a strategy that came to be known as the "no-cities doctrine." The essence of the plan was that should the two superpowers find themselves in a nuclear war, each should strive to concentrate its fire on the opponent's military forces and spare its cities.

The only problem with the proposed strategy was that if the United States had enough nuclear delivery systems with the requisite accuracies to pinpoint and destroy Soviet weapons and military installations in retaliation to an attack, it might also have enough muscle to do the same thing in a first strike. That might be perfectly acceptable to Washington, but from Moscow's perspective, such a situation would be a disaster. In response, the Kremlin would seek to proliferate its own nuclear forces until it could be certain that some portion of its arsenal would escape destruction and survive to retaliate. For the strategy to work, the United States would have to stay ahead of this numbers game indefinitely. It was a prescription for a costly and open-ended arms race. In addition, there was no assurance that the United States would win such a contest. Finally, as the Soviet Union began to deploy its ICBMs in blast resistent underground silos and to place more and more missiles at sea in submarines, administration military planners recognized that the ability of the United States to destroy all of the Kremlin's nuclear forces in a surgically precise counterforce attack would soon become a technical impossibility, even with the forces scheduled to come on line.

For these reasons, McNamara and the administration ultimately settled on a strategy that had at its core the notion of assured destruction. Twenty years after its introduction into our vocabulary, the phrase still provokes controversy and heated debate. "Assured destruction" is not so much a military doctrine, as many of its opponents have claimed, as it is a condition. Reduced to its essence, it refers to the reality, apparent as early as 1964-65, that in the event of nuclear war involving the United States and the Soviet Union, neither could hope to prevail in any meaningful sense, as the side struck first would very likely retain enough nuclear weapons to inflict, in response, a level of destruction that the aggressor would regard as unacceptable. The development of ballistic missiles, as discussed in Chapter 2, had made it virtually impossible for either superpower to defend itself reliably against a nuclear attack. Consequently, the basis of deterrence became not the power to defeat one's adversary by blunting his attack (either through defensive measures or by striking first), but by having the ability to "ride out" the aggression and then to deliver a crippling counterblow—at least as devastating in its effects as the enemy's initial attack.

Assured destruction had two important implications. First, strict adherence to its logic should have eliminated the need to maintain nuclear superiority. For deterrence of this kind to work effectively, country A need only deploy a limited number of nuclear weapons in ways that could not be targeted and destroyed by country B. That number could be anything from several hundred to several thousand, depending on the desired level of destruction. Beyond a certain threshold, however, additional weapons would be of marginal utility, as most of the damage against population centers, industrial facilities, transportation centers, and the like would have been inflicted by the first 500 to 1000 weapons.

Second, the preferred situation would be one in which both adversaries subscribed to the assured destruction model. If one did and the other didn't—that is, if one rushed to acquire the forces to prevail while the other contented itself with a minimum deterrence posture—great pressures would be generated on the second to keep pace, if only for psychological reasons and to reassure its own population. Especially destabilizing in this context would be an effort by either or both of the superpowers to combine large-scale investments in offensive forces with measures to limit population and industrial damage through such "active" mechanisms as defenses against bombers and missiles and more "passive" steps, including civil defense. In the perverse logic of assured destruction, a country prepared to defend itself is a country to be feared. Defensive measures could be interpreted by the other side as an indication of warlike intent.

Despite NcNamara's eventual endorsement of assured destruction, the United States acquired offensive nuclear forces that far surpassed the requirements of minimum deterrence. The Kennedy administration's general support for a strong defense posture, coupled with continuing Congressional anxiety over the Soviet "threat" and the Pentagon's commitment to field the best and the most weapons systems possible, combined to give this country by the mid-1960s a nuclear arsenal several times as large as that of the Soviet Union. It has been estimated, for example, that at the time of the Cuban missile crisis U.S. strategic nuclear forces outnumbered those of the Kremlin by at least five to one.[4]

The Soviet military buildup began several years after the start of the American expansion. From the late 1950s to 1963, Soviet nuclear forces grew much more slowly than some American intelligence agencies had predicted. The reasons remain somewhat obscure, but probably had to do with technical shortcomings in the early types of Soviet land-based missiles that made large-scale procurements unattractive. It may also have been a consequence of budgetary constraints; Khrushchev had ordered a reduction in the size of the Soviet army and a cutback in naval procurements in 1960.[5] Although the Strategic Rocket Forces, created in December 1959, received preferential treatment from the Soviet leader, actual military funding levels may have declined or stayed the same until 1961, when a series of international crises convinced Khrushchev to abandon his defense austerity drive.

In any event, large numbers of silo-based Soviet ICBMs did not begin to appear until after Khrushchev's ouster in October 1964. Once under way, however, the buildup was impressive. In the following five years, the Kremlin deployed approximately 800 long-range land-based missiles and several hundred modern submarine-based systems. By the end of 1969, the combined total of Soviet ICBMs and SLBMs was 1200, only 500 fewer than the United States had amassed. Moreover, the Soviets were building new missiles at the rate of over 300 per year.[6] The U.S. program had topped out in 1967 at 1054 ICBMs and 656 SLBMs. The Soviets also invested heavily during these years in an elaborate air-defense system for protection against American bombers and began work on an anti-ballistic missile network around Moscow.

These latter developments strongly suggested that whatever the implications for strategic stability, Kremlin leaders were determined to provide Soviet society at least some degree of protection against American nuclear weapons. Expressed differently, the Soviets appeared to reject the idea that the most reliable way to deter a nuclear war was through the reciprocal capacity of the superpowers to inflict "unacceptable damage" in response to an attack. At this stage at least, the Kremlin seemed more interested in acquiring the requisite forces to prevail.

Simultaneous with the effort to accelerate the buildup in strategic nuclear forces, the Kennedy administration also undertook a careful reexamination of NATO's military doctrine. It had become conventional wisdom by the late 1950s that the Atlantic alliance was unprepared for war in Europe. Should such a conflict arise, experts warned, Western military forces would be unable to contain a Warsaw Pact offensive without the early and extensive use of nuclear weapons. Consequently, any war in Europe could quickly get out of hand, possibly escalating to a strategic nuclear exchange between the superpowers within a matter of days, if not hours. To forestall such an eventuality, the president and his senior advisers pressed the allies to adopt a new strategy, one that would equip NATO forces with a wider range of military options.

The most effective way to deter a European conflict, the Americans argued, was to have forces in being that could respond in a proportionate manner to the provocation at hand. If the Warsaw Pact attacked with conventional forces, for example, the West should be in a position to defend itself, at least initially, at roughly the same level of violence. Moreover, if the fighting grew more intense, NATO should have the resources to keep pace. The ability of the Atlantic Alliance to respond in this way, U.S. strategists seemed to believe, could dissuade the Soviets from attacking in the first place—as at the end of this ladder of escalation was the American strategic arsenal, which, in the early 1960s, was several times as powerful as that belonging to the Kremlin. The new doctrine was called "flexible response."[7]

Much of NATO Europe was less than enthusiastic about the projected change in strategy. Not only would flexible response be more costly than the existing posture, requiring additional outlays for personnel and equipment, but it might also increase rather than the decrease the likelihood of war. If the Soviet Union and its allies could attack Western Europe with some confidence that the war would remain non-nuclear, might they not be more tempted to strike? Having suffered through a disastrous war not twenty years before, many Europeans were less interested in preparing to fight a full-scale military campaign on the continent than in deterring one. For some in Europe, it was precisely the incalculable risks associated with nuclear weapons that made them such an excellent deterrent. The Soviets would have to be mad to attack the West, according to this reasoning, knowing in advance that NATO's only recourse would be to authorize the use of its nuclear forces.

The debate continued for some time within NATO councils and was not resolved until 1967, when the alliance finally endorsed a watered-down version of flexible response. As with most controversial issues, each party to the negotiations settled for something less than what it would have preferred. The United States got Western Europe's commitment to do more by way of conventional defense and the allies received a strong reaffirmation of Washington's nuclear

Kennedy and Khrushchev met in Vienna in June 1961, seven weeks after CIA-trained Cuban exiles had attempted to provoke an uprising and overthrow Castro. Their encounter was tense and the meeting accomplished little.

guarantee. While NATO's war-fighting posture improved during the 1960s, it was never so enhanced as to provide the West with a genuine conventional military option.

The Bay of Pigs, the Crisis in Berlin, and the Missiles in Cuba

In 1961, both flexible response and the administration's strategic weapons buildup still lay in the future. It is true, nonetheless, that the crises which erupted during the first two years of the Kennedy administration took place against a backdrop of general U.S. military superiority. It was, however, a superiority that the young Democratic president and his advisers had a difficult time manipulating to U.S. advantage.

In April 1961, some 1500 Cuban exiles, trained and equipped by the Central Intelligence Agency, stormed ashore along several southern beaches of that Caribbean island in an attempt to provoke a general uprising and overthrow Castro. The attack encountered stiff Communist resistance; only the introduction of U.S. airpower might have saved the operation. Kennedy ruled against an American air strike, as well as other forms of direct U.S. assistance, and the exiles were quickly defeated. The president had decided that the risks associated with American intervention were simply too great. Seven weeks later, Kennedy met Khrushchev in Vienna. It was not a particularly amicable encounter. Kennedy was reported to have come away slightly unnerved from his only face-to-face session with the Soviet leader.

In August, for the third time since World War II, Berlin became the focus of superpower tension as Khrushchev announced his intention (later abandoned) to sign a treaty with the German Democratic Republic officially concluding World War II. Among other things, this treaty would leave the administration of the eastern half of that divided city in East German rather than Soviet hands. The message seemed to be that American, British, and French access rights to West Berlin would have to be renegotiated with the GDR. Also in August, the Communists erected a wall through the heart of the former German capital, ostensibly to protect East Berliners from possible Western aggression but in reality to stem the flight of East German citizens to the western parts of the city. The wall constituted a violation of the World War II agreement governing the status of Berlin, which had stipulated that the city would be administered as a single unit. Although they would have been within their legal rights to do so, the United States, the United Kingdom, and France chose not to confront the Soviets over the construction of the wall and Berlin became, for all intents and purposes, two cities—one Communist and one Western.

Khrushchev may have thought himself on something of a roll in foreign policy despite, from his perspective, the disadvantageous character of the strategic military balance between the superpowers. On the assumption that the Americans would grumble but not actively oppose the placement of Soviet medium- and intermediate-range ballistic missiles in Cuba, Khrushchev set out to improve the Soviet military position vis-à-vis the United States. Aspects of the missile crisis have already been considered in Chapter 2. Suffice it to say in this context that the Soviet leader miscalculated, provoking the most dangerous confrontation between Moscow and Washington before or since. For thirteen days, the spectre of nuclear war hung over the world like the proverbial sword of Damocles. In the end, Khrushchev retreated, agreeing to withdraw the missiles in exchange for an American pledge not to invade Castro's Cuba.

MRBM LAUNCH SITE 3
SAN CRISTOBAL, CUBA
27 OCTOBER 1962

LAUNCH AREA

NUCLEAR WARHEAD BUNKER U/C

PERMANENT BLDGS

OPEN STORAGE

TRENCH

American reconnaissance photographs revealed the deployment of Soviet nuclear forces in Cuba.

For twenty-four years, Western analysts have speculated as to why, in the words of former Secretary of State Dean Rusk, the Soviets "blinked" first during the Cuban crisis. Certainly, the reality of American nuclear superiority weighed heavily in Khrushchev's calculations. Had a nuclear war erupted between the superpowers in October 1962, the Soviet Union would have been devastated. The United States, in all likelihood, would have sustained relatively less damage (although attacks against certain American cities would have been enormously destructive). In addition, the local and non-nuclear balance of military power in the region strongly favored the United States. In other words, in a confrontation between Soviet and Cuban forces, on the one hand, and the U.S. military power, on the other, the outcome would never have been in doubt. Faced with the certainty of defeat should the crisis escalate, Khrushchev chose a negotiated settlement, restoring the status quo ante.

The resolution of the Cuban missile crisis brought to an end two and a half years of palpable tension in U.S.-Soviet relations. In the wake of that dramatic episode, the two superpowers consciously sought a limited detente that made possible two modest but significant arms control agreements: the Limited Test Ban Treaty of August 1963 and the establishment of the Hotline. The latter, although less visible in its effects, may have been the more important. The Hotline, which enabled American and Soviet leaders to communicate with one another directly by means of a teletype machine, underscored the recognition on both sides that nuclear weapons had transformed the nature of their competition, placing real if imprecise limits on the range of permissible behavior. It symbolized the fact that mutual action could be required to guard against the possibility that through accident or miscalculation the two superpowers could find themselves at war. It offered some evidence in support of the proposition that political leaders in both countries were coming to accept the view that a nuclear exchange could not be won—at least not in the way the term had traditionally been employed and not at that particular point in time. In all fairness, however, there was other evidence, such as the Kremlin's heavy investment in strategic defensive capabilities, that seemed to suggest the opposite conclusion.

The outcome of the crisis in Cuba also must have played a part in convincing the Soviet leadership to expend whatever resources might be necessary to attain, at a minimum, a position of strategic military equality with the United States. That decision may have been taken before the Cuban debacle. We have no way of knowing for sure. Were there any doubts concerning the wisdom of doing so, however, they must have evaporated in the wake of the Soviet humiliation. Khrushchev was unceremoniously dumped from the Politburo in October 1964 for his part in the crisis and for other controversial decisions, ranging from his forced reorganization of the Communist Party apparatus to his high-risk economic policies.

The death of President Kennedy in November 1963 and the ouster of Khrushchev eleven months later coincided with yet another downturn in superpower relations, as American policymakers shifted their attention to the widening war in Southeast Asia and Khrushchev's successors adopted a Stalin-like posture of hostility toward the United States. For two years—from 1965 to 1967—the relationship remained at this low ebb.

Stirrings in Arms Control

In June 1967 a meeting between President Johnson and Soviet Premier Alexei Kosygin in Glassboro, New Jersey, signaled a slight improvement in relations. Part of their discussion centered on the nuclear arms race and what might be done to control it. Of special concern to the United States was the Soviet deployment, then in progress, of the anti-ballistic missile system around Moscow. The president and Secretary of Defense McNamara emphasized the nature of the U.S. concern at this development, stressing that the Kremlin's apparent interest in ABM technologies could introduce a new and destabilizing factor into the military relationship between the superpowers. Specifically, Johnson and McNamara warned, the United States might be forced to respond in kind to Soviet efforts, setting off a new round in the arms competition that would leave both sides worse off than before.[8]

The Secretary of Defense also went to considerable lengths to explain why the construction of elaborate strategic defenses, dedicated to the protection of cities, would merely encourage the proliferation of additional offensive weapons, as the ultimate source of each country's security was its power to retaliate effectively to an attack. Put simply, strategic defenses, if deployed widely, could call into question the other side's "assured destruction" capability, thereby undermining rather than enhancing deterrence.

The Soviets initially resisted this line of argument, contending that actions taken to defend people from the effects of a nuclear war could not be considered inconsistent with preserving peace; moreover, proper defensive preparations were the obligation of any government concerned with the well-being of its citizens. Soviet thinking began to change when McNamara, in a speech on September 18, 1967, announced the U.S. intention to deploy a limited though nationwide ABM system, called Sentinel. The purposes of Sentinel, according to the administration, were to protect Americans against an eventual Chinese nuclear threat, as well as an accidental or unauthorized launch of Soviet ICBMs. Whatever the rationale, the Kremlin understood that, once completed, an American ABM network would enjoy at least some capability to deflect a Soviet nuclear strike (either preemptive or retaliatory), thereby endangering its nuclear deterrent. To make matters worse, "limited" defenses could always be expanded and upgraded at a later date. Lastly, the Soviets may have concluded that in a wide open race between the two superpowers in the development and deployment of anti-ballistic missile systems, the United States might emerge distinctly better off militarily, given its larger and more advanced technical base.

A second reason for the Kremlin's emerging interest in strategic arms control was the approach of nuclear parity between the superpowers. In 1968, Soviet forces, while still less numerous than those of the United States, were growing rapidly. Rough equality was, from the Soviet perspective, a prerequisite for serious negotiations. It was also within reach for the first time. From Washington's vantage point, curtailing the further expansion of the Kremlin's nuclear arsenal and reaching an agreement to bar large-scale ABM deployments were becoming important policy objectives. For the first time since the dawn of the nuclear age, in other words, the necessary preconditions for entering into comprehensive arms control negotiations appeared to be at hand.

In July 1968, the United States and the Soviet Union announced their willingness to explore the possibility of concluding limits on their offensive and defensive strategic forces. Plans were made to initiate discussions at a summit meeting between President Johnson and Premier Kosygin, scheduled to begin on September 30 in Leningrad. On August 21, Soviet and Warsaw Pact forces invaded Czechoslovakia. In reponse, the U.S. government called off the meeting with Kosygin and suspended preparations for the negotiations.

Having finally convinced—or coerced—the Soviets to explore the delicate issue of nuclear arms control, Johnson felt he had no option but to abandon his plans in the wake of the Czech crisis, leaving to his Republican successor, Richard Nixon, the decision whether to pursue the matter. It must have grieved Johnson to do so, in light of his own concerns about his place in history as well as Nixon's reputation as an unreconstructed Cold Warrior. He had no way of knowing, of course, that it would be Nixon and his German-born national security adviser, Henry Kissinger, who would stage-manage the transition in U.S.-Soviet relations from confrontation to detente.

What's the Key? / *Lanny Sommese*

5 The Detente Experiment 1969–1980

In the beginning it seemed simple enough and eminently reasonable. The United States and the Soviet Union, it was announced in October 1969, would soon begin negotiations to limit their strategic nuclear arsenals. Two and a half years later, in Moscow, Richard Nixon and Leonid Brezhnev signed the first of several arms control agreements. Others were to follow, including two treaties restricting underground nuclear weapons testing and, in 1979, a more comprehensive accord—the ill-fated SALT II agreement—that promised for the first time in postwar history to reduce the number of U.S. and Soviet nuclear weapon systems. During the halcyon days of detente, between 1971 and 1974, the two superpowers also concluded a series of political agreements that together seemed to provide a kind of road map for the future positive development of relations and for the mutually beneficial resolution of disputes.

By the end of the 1970s, however, this first sustained effort at regulating the military and, to a lesser extent, the political competition between Washington and Moscow lay in shambles. Detente, a word that most elected American officials had been only too eager to employ during the early part of the decade, had become by the time of the 1980 presidential election a term of derision in the United States. To be perceived as a supporter of detente and negotiated arms control during the last two years of Jimmy Carter's single term was to court political disaster. Candidate Ronald Reagan campaigned vigorously and successfully against both the policy of detente and the 1979 Strategic Arms Limitation treaty, which he consistently characterized as "fatally flawed." While owing his election to a variety of factors—ranging from high interest rates to frustration over the seizure of U.S. embassy officials in Tehran—Reagan's victory was also symptomatic of the abrupt decline in detente's popular appeal. By 1981, what Nixon had once and rather grandiloquently described as "the emerging structure for peace" had all but collapsed and been eclipsed by a new and intense round of superpower hostility that rivaled (rhetorically at least) the worst days of the Cold War.

Coming to a reasoned, balanced, dispassionate, and historically accurate assessment of detente is a difficult task. To begin with, its scope is immense and its history enormously complicated. One recent and quite excellent study of U.S.-Soviet relations between 1969 and 1981 is over 1100 pages long;[1] literally scores of books, some scholarly and some less so, have been written on one or another dimension of detente since the mid-1970s. In addition, most of the U.S. documentation essential for a thorough analysis of the period is classified and will remain so for many years to come, and Soviet sources may never be available. Finally, detente evokes strong feelings; many Americans hold quite definite opinions on the subject. At one extreme are those who argue that detente was an important opportunity to redirect superpower relations from confrontation to cooperation—an opportunity that was squandered by shortsighted politicians in Washington and Moscow unable to resist the temptation to exploit the other side's weaknesses and perceived vulnerabilities. At the other extreme are those who charge that detente was a well laid Soviet plan to ensnare the United States in a series of disadvantageous arms control agreements and diplomatic "understandings," all of which were designed to erode its military power and political influence. Most Americans, with varying degrees of assurance and conviction, hold views that fall somewhere in between.

The purpose of this chapter is not to recount the history of U.S.-Soviet detente. Rather, it is to place the experience in perspective, extracting from the historical record those lessons or insights that contribute to an understanding of the superpower relationship as a whole. What was the essence of detente and how did the United States and the Soviet Union perceive its purpose? What factors contributed to its rise and why did it collapse? How important was the military balance between the superpowers in facilitating the relaxation of political tensions? What role did arms control play? In the end, what are we to make of this relatively brief experience that began so well and ended so badly?

At root, detente was a collaborative effort to regulate certain aspects of the superpower relationship within a larger context of continuing rivalry. It was not, in other words, an attempt to eliminate or to negotiate away the causes of that competition. Leaders in both countries operated on the assumption that U.S.-Soviet relations were and would remain fundamentally adversarial in nature. The goal, therefore, was never to foster friendship per se or to replace antagonism with alliance. Nor was detente, as sometimes charged, a Soviet strategy to engineer the United States into accepting a position of permanent military and political inferiority, reluctantly embraced by an American leadership too demoralized and preoccupied to resist. To argue this way is to suggest that during this period the Kremlin enjoyed such a preponderance of power as to compel the United States to accept an outcome inimical to its interests. Throughout the 1970s, the strategic nuclear forces of the two sides were roughly equal in size and capability; neither country enjoyed anything approaching usable military superiority.

The essential core of detente was arms control. What enabled Washington and Moscow to achieve a general if short-lived relaxation in political tensions was the decision to seek negotiated constraints on their strategic nuclear forces. That decision was the result of hardheaded calculations in both countries. American policymakers concluded that, given the sheer number of weapons and the inadequacy of defensive measures, meaningful nuclear superiority—defined as the ability to prevail over the adversary in the event of war—could not be maintained. Soviet leaders appeared to reach much the same conclusion, although, at least in the early years, their principal interest in arms control appears to have been more political than military. The formal recognition of military equality between the superpowers, the Soviets seemed to believe, was a necessary precondition to Moscow's realization of essential political equality with Washington. The American conception of detente also had an important political dimension, although perhaps less developed at the outset and certainly less explicit than the Soviet vision.

When detente began to unravel toward the end of the 1970s, it was the erosion of U.S. confidence in negotiated arms control as a device to restrain the further growth and development of Soviet military power that, more than any other single factor, compelled a reexamination of policy. Far from stabilizing the military situation between the superpowers, critics alleged, arms control had introduced new elements of instability, most notably the utilization by the Soviet Union of various loopholes in the agreements to expand and to modernize its nuclear forces. The United States, on the other hand, had restrained the development of its military forces in conformity with the accords and in the expectation that the Kremlin would reciprocate. Such, at least, was the bill of particulars leveled against what came to be known collectively as SALT, or the Strategic Arms Limitation Talks.

Other factors contributed to the decline of detente, of course, including the Kremlin's military involvement in Africa, the Soviet invasion of Afghanistan, and a generalized disappointment on the part of U.S. policymakers at Moscow's failure to demonstrate greater "restraint" in the conduct of its foreign policy. But these were of secondary importance. President Carter's national security adviser, Zbigniew Brzezinski, wrote at one point late in the administration that the second strategic arms limitation agreement, signed in 1979 but never ratified by the United States, had fallen prey to the deterioration in superpower political relations. SALT, Brzezinski argued, "lies buried in the sands of the Ogaden" (the desert region of eastern Ethiopia), the reference being to the Soviet Union's active military assistance to the Ethiopian regime in its war with Somalia and the impact of that intervention on American expert and public opinion.[2] In actuality, SALT was in trouble long before the first Soviet soldier set foot on Ethiopian soil and its problems derived only to a modest extent from the increase in Moscow's political and military activism in the Third World. In the end, what undermined the basis for progress in arms control and brought an end to the detente experiment was the conviction held by both Washington and Moscow that the other was bent on achieving military superiority.

The Rise and Fall of Detente

Detente came about because U.S. and Soviet leaders saw it in their interest to limit or constrain various aspects of their competition. On the American side, the incentives to seek a modest improvement in relations with Moscow were several. Richard Nixon came to office in January 1969 arguing that the time had come to initiate an era of negotiation, seeming to suggest that such rigid Cold War formulas as Truman-style containment had outlived their usefulness as mechanisms to address the modern challenges posed by the Soviet Union in particular and by Communism more generally.

Uppermost in Nixon's mind at the time was the attainment of a negotiated settlement of the war in Vietnam that would allow for a graceful U.S. exit and an honorable peace. Moscow, as one of North Vietnam's principal allies and the major source of its outside military assistance, could be helpful in facilitating such an outcome. Nixon and his national security adviser, Henry Kissinger, were also eager to exploit to American advantage the very real tensions between the Soviet Union and China that had emerged in recent years and that would soon result in a series of border clashes between the two Communist giants along the Ussuri and Amur Rivers, including one particularly violent incident in March 1969. Improving relations with both countries could increase American bargaining leverage with each.

From the Soviet perspective, a reduction in superpower tensions might make possible a further improvement in relations with America's NATO allies—by 1969 an important goal of the Kremlin's foreign policy. In particular, Soviet leaders were eager to attain Western recognition of the postwar "gains of socialism," including a multilateral confirmation of the territorial and political changes in Eastern Europe that had come about as a consequence of World War II. An all-European security conference was much more likely to be convened with American acquiescence than without it. Better relations with the United States might also result in increased bilateral trade and the easing of restrictions on the importation of advanced American industrial technology, steps which could be of enormous value in modernizing the Soviet economy. In addition, by making detente conditional on an American posture of benign neglect toward China, Moscow could make it much harder for the United States to seek closer relations with its most populous rival.

Different though equally strong incentives to improve superpower relations had existed in the past. And yet, with few exceptions, such as the slight warming in relations following the Cuban missile crisis that made possible the conclusion of the Limited Test Ban Treaty and the installation of the Hotline, nothing lasting or substantial had been achieved. At each turn, the political factors working toward at least a partial relaxation of tensions had been short-circuited by the continuing military rivalry between the superpowers. This time would be different. The interesting question is why?

Before committing himself to the initiation of strategic arms limitation talks that had first been proposed during the last year of the Johnson administration and to which the Soviets had responded positively, President Nixon authorized a comprehensive review of U.S. defense policy; later in 1969, he and Kissinger also prodded the bureaucracy to assess the implications for U.S. security of negotiating with Moscow an agreement or agreements to control strategic nuclear forces.[3] At the time of these studies, the American nuclear arsenal had stabilized at approximately 1700 land- and sea-based missiles, and 400 long-range bombers. Soviet nuclear forces, by contrast, were growing rapidly. From a position of marked strategic inferiority as late as 1963, the Kremlin by 1969 was rapidly approaching rough numerical equality. Whether the Soviets would be satisfied with parity or would build beyond that level was a mystery to American planners. Along with their offensive forces, the two sides had under way strategic defensive programs designed to intercept incoming ballistic missile warheads. The Soviet effort, deployed around Moscow, was nearing operational readiness; work on the American system, reoriented in 1969 to protect missile silos rather than cities, lagged several years behind and had yet to be fully funded by Congress.

Against this backdrop, the administration completed its review of defense policy, known as National Security Study Memorandum 3. The report's findings were important at the time and little in the seventeen years since their release has diminished their significance. Among its conclusions, the report found that meaningful nuclear superiority could not be maintained against a country with the military and economic capabilities of the Soviet Union. In the place of superiority, the report urged "sufficiency" and "essential equivalence" as guides to the sizing of U.S. strategic forces. In other words, the primary mission of the U.S. nuclear arsenal should be to deter Soviet aggression against this country and its allies under any and all conditions—and not to win a nuclear war. The report made no attempt to spell out the precise requirements of "sufficiency" at this stage, an omission that, however understandable, was later to complicate negotiations not only with Moscow but also between the administration and Congress.[4]

The review also concluded that an effective ABM defense of the United States would not only be technically impossible, but, given the likely impact of a competition in this area between the two superpowers, destabilizing as well. Because ABM systems would cost more "at the margin" than the procurement of additional offensive forces, both countries would have a strong incentive to proliferate the latter, thereby maintaining their respective assured destruction capabilities. Furthermore, building more and more ABM installations to keep pace with the increase in missile forces would be enormously expensive and ultimately of limited value, inasmuch as only a small proportion of U.S. or Soviet nuclear weapons would need to arrive on target to inflict unprecedented levels of damage against the other side. Finally, the review suggested that the time was propitious for serious bilateral negotiations to limit the offensive forces of the two superpowers, as the number of Soviet ICBMs and SLBMs would be likely to equal those of the United States within the next several years.

It is difficult to exaggerate the importance of these administration findings. The rejection of nuclear superiority as a goal of American military policy, coupled with the imminent arrival of nuclear parity, opened up the possibility for the first time of concluding with Moscow some kind of agreement to regulate the nuclear competition. What remained to be seen was whether the Soviet Union was prepared to enter into negotiations with the new administration and, if so, on what basis and with what objectives.

Moscow was in fact eager to begin the process, communicating its willingness to initiate discussions early in 1969. The first exploratory round of the negotiations convened in Geneva in November of that year. Of special concern to the Kremlin was the negotiation of limits on ABM systems, as specified in an early statement by Vladimir Semenov, chairman of the Soviet SALT delegation. The senior Soviet negotiator drew attention to the ambiguous character of modern nuclear weaponry when he noted that "offensive" forces could be considered defensive if they served to deter the outbreak of war; "defensive" forces, he contended, could be seen as offensive in character if either side were to contemplate their use in order to frustrate an adversary's retaliatory strike. It was a nearly complete reversal of the argument put forth by Premier Kosygin during his brief meeting with President Johnson in 1967. Semenov's characterization of antiballistic missiles as potentially destabilizing was consistent with the American view and a strong signal that Moscow and Washington were on the same wavelength, at least on this issue.[5]

Semenov also admitted that a situation of mutual deterrence existed between the superpowers; in the event one side were to be attacked, he noted, the victim of aggression would still retain sufficient forces to retaliate. As a consequence, the country striking first would be committing suicide. On this point, too, the two countries appeared to be in agreement.

Whether Washington and Moscow could agree on measures to limit the size of their strategic offensive forces was less apparent. On the one hand, the Soviet Union's seeming endorsement of mutual deterrence—meaning that both sides were and would continue to be utterly vulnerable to retaliation—suggested that a deal might be possible. On the other hand, American bargaining leverage on this issue was less than impressive as U.S. nuclear forces had topped out several years before with no plans to increase the number of missiles or bombers. The Soviets, in contrast, were still building new systems at an impressive rate.

The ABM Treaty and the Interim Agreement on Offensive Forces

In May 1971, the two countries announced that they would pursue two agreements during this first round of SALT. The first would be a treaty to limit severely the deployment of ABM systems. The second would be an accord to impose certain constraints on the further growth and development of offensive forces. A year later, at the Moscow summit, both agreements were signed. The ABM treaty restricted each side to two anti-ballistic missile installations (later reduced to one), both quite limited in scope, and obligated the parties "not to deploy ABM systems for a defense of the territory of its country and not to provide a base for such a defense. . . ."[6] Other provisions, equally restrictive, regulated the narrow band of permissible activities. The treaty was of unlimited duration, although both parties reserved the right to withdraw from the agreement on six months' notice, should "supreme interests" dictate.

Reduced to its essence, the treaty codified the mutuality of deterrence, based on the logic of assured destruction. As long as both countries adhered to its provisions, neither could mount an effective nationwide defense against missile-borne nuclear weapons. Moreover, neither would be allowed to try. Other actions might be undertaken to limit damage in the event of war, such as civil defense procedures and defenses against manned bombers, but in the absence of a national ABM network, the effectiveness of these measures would remain problematic at best. The ABM treaty reflected the judgment on the part of both countries that whatever they might prefer in the abstract, their mutual vulnerability to nuclear retaliation was a fact that could not be undone through technical means, at least for the time being. It also symbolized the recognition that the best safeguard against nuclear war, again for the foreseeable future, was the preservation of that vulnerability.

The accord on the limitation of offensive forces was a partial freeze on key strategic nuclear delivery vehicles, each side agreeing not to build additional ICBM and SLBM launchers (silos and missile tubes) beyond those already in existence or under construction at the time of the signing.[7] Moscow was permitted, however, on a one-time basis, to add up to 210 submarine-launched missiles to its arsenal by retiring an equal number of older land-based missiles. The so-called Interim Agreement produced a balance in missile forces favoring the Kremlin (2300 to 1700), although it did not limit the number of long-range bombers, an area in which the United States enjoyed a substantial numerical advantage (approximately 400 to 150). Even so, the accord was criticized in the United States for granting the Kremlin at least the appearance of military superiority, however meaningless that concept had become in an age of nuclear overkill.

The agreement also set some loose parameters around the introduction of new land-based missiles and the modernization of existing types. In addition, Moscow undertook not to deploy additional "heavy" ICBMs, an issue of considerable importance to American negotiators because of the ability of these weapons to launch large payloads, including extremely high-yield warheads. Another provision affirmed the right of the parties to monitor compliance with the terms of the agreement through so-called national technical means, such as satellite reconnaissance and electronic eavesdropping. The ABM treaty contained a similar clause. On-site inspection was considered unnecessary. The Interim Agreement was to last five years or until a follow-up and more comprehensive accord could be concluded.

The Interim Agreement suffered from significant shortcomings, most of which were recognized at the time. The problem of "unequal force aggregates," the exclusion of bombers, and the lack of precision concerning permissible ICBM modernization have already been noted. In addition, the accord failed to impose limits on the development, procurement, or deployment of multiple independently-targetable reentry vehicles, or MIRVs. The United States chose not to press for a ban on multiple-warhead technology because it was considered to be one way to compensate for the Soviet advantage in missile numbers. MIRVs were also an area in which the United States was believed to enjoy a 4- to 5-year technological lead over the Soviet Union—which might constitute an important bargaining lever in later negotiations. The Kremlin was not particularly enthusiastic about stopping MIRVs either, as the United States had already initiated the testing of such systems in the year prior to the start of the negotiations; in 1970, Washington had begun to deploy the Minuteman III ICBM, each armed with three warheads. A ban on procurement and deployment at that late date would have left the United States in sole possession of a proven technology and of some number of operational multiple-warhead ICBMs. Better to do nothing at all, the Soviets may have reasoned, than to deny themselves a capability already attained by their negotiating partner. The decision not to forgo the MIRV option would come back to haunt the American side.

When the administration submitted the two agreements for Congressional approval during the summer of 1972, the ABM treaty secured the necessary Senate ratification easily. The Interim Agreement, on the other hand, encountered some opposition. Although not a treaty, the accord was put before both houses of Congress for debate and consideration. In the end the measure was approved by a lopsided majority in the House and Senate but not before passage of a nonbinding sense-of-the-Congress resolution, sponsored by Senator Henry Jackson of Washington, stipulating that in future negotiations the United States should insist on the principle of equality and refuse to accept "inferior [force] levels." Obviously, not everyone in the American government was entirely comfortable with the administration's notions of strategic sufficiency and "essential equivalence." Two years later, in a statement of principles drafted during the meeting between Brezhnev and President Gerald Ford in the Soviet city of Vladivostok, the two sides agreed that a second SALT treaty should include equal numerical limits on strategic offensive forces.[8]

During the 1972 summit, Nixon and Brezhnev also put their names to a rather curious document known as the Basic Principles of Relations. In it, the two leaders pledged to base U.S.-Soviet relations on the principles of peaceful coexistence, to eschew the pursuit of unilateral advantage, to conduct discussions and negotiations in a spirit of "reciprocity, mutual accommodation and mutual benefit," and to renounce the use or threat of force in their bilateral diplomacy. Had it been honored by the two sides—which it was not—it could have gone a long way toward reducing superpower political tensions and creating new opportunities for cooperation beyond the narrow confines of arms control. To expect Washington and Moscow to abide by all of its provisions to the letter, however, was to ignore much of postwar history and their continuing global rivalry. The American side never accorded it much importance, regarding it as more an example of Moscow's fondness for high-sounding rhetoric and purple prose than as a true framework for the future development of superpower relations. In contrast, the Soviets seemed to view it as one of the central accomplishments of the summit, seldom failing to mention it when recounting the contributions of detente to the maintenance of international peace and security.[9]

The overarching problem with the Basic Principles of Relations agreement was, to use a Soviet phrase, how to "infuse it with content." A satisfactory answer was never forthcoming. The agreement remained a hollow pledge, violated by both sides. From the perspective of the 1980s, it is perhaps the most confusing legacy of detente. To some observers it was a testament to the willingness of U.S. and Soviet leaders to set their relationship on a new and more positive footing. To others, it was a cynical gesture, an example of superpower duplicity at its worst. Typically, the truth lies somewhere in the middle.

The Politics of Linkage

The apparent superpower success in arms control, together with the overall improvement in relations that accompanied the signing of the ABM treaty and the Interim Agreement, spawned a number of additional initiatives and negotiations in such areas as cultural exchanges, scientific and technological cooperation, and trade. Of these, the development of economic relations held special importance for the Kremlin. Eager to accelerate the transition from *extensive* to *intensive* economic development, the Soviet Union looked to American technology to assist in that process. U.S. businessmen were interested in providing the necessary equipment, along with related services. To facilitate such trade, the administration appealed to Congress to extend to Moscow most-favored-nation status (MFN) and a large line of credit through the U.S. Export-Import Bank. In what was to become a persistent feature of detente and a particularly divisive issue between the superpowers, Congress insisted on link-

Basic Principles of Relations Between the United States of America and the Union of Soviet Socialist Republics, May 29, 1972

The United States of America and the Union of Soviet Socialist Republics,

Guided by their obligations under the Charter of the United Nations and by a desire to strengthen peaceful relations with each other and to place these relations on the firmest possible basis,

Aware of the need to make every effort to remove the threat of war and to create conditions which promote the reduction of tensions in the world and the strengthening of universal security and international cooperation,

Believing that the improvement of US-Soviet relations and their mutually advantageous development in such areas as economics, science and culture, will meet these objectives and contribute to better mutual understanding and business-like cooperation, without in any way prejudicing the interests of third countries,

Conscious that these objectives reflect the interests of the people of both countries,

Have agreed as follows:

First. They will proceed from the common determination that in the nuclear age there is no alternative to conducting their mutual relations on the basis of peaceful coexistence. Differences in ideology and in the social systems of the USA and the USSR are not obstacles to the bilateral development of normal relations based on the principles of sovereignty, equality, non-interference in internal affairs and mutual advantage.

Second. The USA and the USSR attach major importance to preventing the development of situations capable of causing a dangerous exacerbation of their relations. Therefore, they will do their utmost to avoid military confrontations and to prevent the outbreak of nuclear war. They will always exercise restraint in their mutual relations, and will be prepared to negotiate and settle differences by peaceful means. Discussions and negotiations on outstanding issues will be conducted in a spirit of reciprocity, mutual accommodation and mutual benefit.

Both sides recognize that efforts to obtain unilateral advantage at the expense of the other, directly or indirectly, are inconsistent with these objectives. The prerequisites for maintaining and strengthening peaceful relations between the USA and the USSR are the recognition of the security interests of the Parties based on the principle of equality and the renunciation of the use or threat of force.

Third. The USA and the USSR have a special responsibility, as do other countries which are permanent members of the United Nations Security Council, to do everything in their power so that conflicts or situations will not arise which would serve to increase international tensions. Accordingly, they will seek to promote conditions in which all countries will live in peace and security and will not be subject to outside interference in their internal affairs.

Fourth. The USA and the USSR intend to widen the juridicial basis of their mutual relations and to exert the necessary efforts so that bilateral agreements which they have concluded and multilateral treaties and agreements to which they are jointly parties are faithfully implemented.

Fifth. The USA and the USSR reaffirm their readiness to continue the practice of exchanging views on problems of mutual interest and, when necessary, to conduct such exchanges at the highest level, including meetings between leaders of the two countries.

The two governments welcome and will facilitate an increase in productive contacts between representatives of the legislative bodies of the two countries.

Sixth. The Parties will continue their efforts to limit armaments on a bilateral as well as on a multilateral basis. They will continue to make special efforts to limit strategic armaments. Whenever possible, they will conclude concrete agreements aimed at achieving these purposes.

The USA and the USSR regard as the ultimate objective of their efforts the achievement of general and complete disarmament and the establishment of an effective system of international security in accordance with the purposes and principles of the United Nations.

Seventh. The USA and the USSR regard commercial and economic ties as an important and necessary element in the strengthening of their bilateral relations and thus will actively promote the growth of such ties. They will facilitate cooperation between the relevant organizations and enterprises of the two countries and the conclusion of appropriate agreements and contracts, including long-term ones.

The two countries will contribute to the improvement of maritime and air communications between them.

Eighth. The two sides consider it timely and useful to develop mutual contacts and cooperation in the fields of science and technology. Where suitable, the USA and the USSR will conclude appropriate agreements dealing with concrete cooperation in these fields.

Ninth. The two sides reaffirm their intention to deepen cultural ties with one another and to encourage fuller familiarization with each other's cultural values. They will promote improved conditions for cultural exchanges and tourism.

Tenth. The USA and the USSR will seek to ensure that their ties and cooperation in all the above-mentioned fields and in any others in their mutual interest are built on a firm and long-term basis. To give a permanent character to these efforts, they will establish in all fields where this is feasible joint commissions or other joint bodies.

Eleventh. The USA and the USSR make no claim for themselves and would not recognize the claims of anyone else to any special rights or advantages in world affairs. They recognize the sovereign equality of all states.

The development of US-Soviet relations is not directed against third countries and their interests.

Twelfth. The basic principles set forth in this document do not affect any obligations with respect to other countries earlier assumed by the USA and the USSR.

Moscow, *May 29, 1972*

For the United States of America	For the Union of Soviet Socialist Republics
RICHARD NIXON	LEONID I. BREZHNEV
President of the United States of America	General Secretary of the Central Committee, CPSU

ing these trade concessions to Soviet emigration policy. If Moscow would adopt a lenient stance with regard to the exodus of Soviet Jews, the United States would grant MFN and open the vault of the Export-Import Bank. If not, the restrictions would remain in force. Late in 1974, Congress passed trade legislation containing these provisions. The Kremlin balked, denouncing the attempt to link trade issues with Soviet emigration practices as gross interference in its internal affairs. As a consequence, the 1972 trade agreement between the United States and the Soviet Union was never enacted. It was the first of many such instances of "linkage" politics in which progress along any one dimension of U.S.-Soviet relations became conditional on progress in a second and sometimes quite separate area. At times, such linkage was explicit, as in the controversy over superpower trade and Jewish emigration. At other times, issues became linked, especially in the United States, because as a practical political matter there was no way to disentangle the different aspects of superpower relations.

The development of detente between Washington and Moscow also contributed to an already active relaxation of tensions in Europe. At the May 1972 summit, for example, the United States agreed to participate in the Conference on Security and Cooperation in Europe (CSCE), the multilateral undertaking that had become a centerpiece of Moscow's European diplomacy and that many of Washington's NATO allies were urging the United States to support as well. In exchange, Washington obtained the Kremlin's pledge to take part in negotiations directed toward a reciprocal reduction in NATO and Warsaw Pact military forces deployed along Europe's central front. Both sets of discussions began within months of the Nixon-Brezhnev meeting.

With hindsight, it is apparent that the U.S.-Soviet detente reached its high-water mark between the first summit and the second, thirteen months later, frictions over trade relations notwithstanding. The SALT negotiations resumed toward the end of 1972 and, at the midpoint of their follow-up meeting in the United States in June 1973, Nixon and Brezhnev signed an agreement obligating the two superpowers to enter into urgent consultations in the event that either country perceived the threat of a nuclear conflict—involving Washington, Moscow, or a third party—to be imminent.

From its modest beginnings in 1969, centered around efforts to control various aspects of the U.S.-Soviet military competition,

Nixon and Brezhnev on the South Portico of the White House at the start of "Summit II" in June 1973.

detente's scope had broadened appreciably by the summer of 1973, touching a wide assortment of issue-areas, ranging from economics and European security to crisis prevention. The real test of detente, however, was not the extent of its reach but the strength of its foundation. How far were the United States and the Soviet Union prepared to go in setting aside the pursuit of unilateral advantage in order to preserve and extend their new relationship?

The Deterioration of Political Relations, 1973-77

The answer came in bits and pieces over the next several years, and for the proponents of detente in both countries the news was not very good. Between 1974 and 1976 the momentum behind the relaxation of political tensions gradually evaporated. In fact, by the time of the 1976 presidential campaign, detente had fallen on such hard times in the United States that President Ford, wrestling with former California Governor Ronald Reagan for the Republican nomination, thought it prudent to excise the term entirely from his political lexicon.

The trouble began in the Middle East, during the Arab-Israeli war of October 1973. At one point in the conflict, as the Israelis (to whom Washington was lending assistance) moved to encircle and destroy the Egyptian Third Army Corps at the southern end of the east bank of the Suez Canal, tensions between the United States and the Soviet Union became acute. The Kremlin, on behalf of its Arab allies, proposed to the United States that the superpowers intervene to enforce a cease-fire; should Washington decline to participate, Moscow left the impression that it was ready to take unilateral action. At about the same time, U.S. intelligence detected higher than usual levels of military activity in several of the U.S.S.R.'s southern military districts. To deter Soviet intervention, the administration prepared to dispatch airborne troops to the Middle East and placed U.S. strategic nuclear forces on alert—knowing full well that Soviet intelligence agencies would inform the political leadership of both steps within hours. At American urging, the Israelis loosened their grip on the trapped Egyptian forces and the crisis passed. Neither Soviet nor American troops were introduced into the region.

Despite the Basic Principles of Relations and the agreement on the prevention of nuclear war, neither of the superpowers made much of an effort to bring the Middle East conflict to a halt during its early stages and each maneuvered to obtain maximum political advantage. Moreover, U.S. officials were chagrined that Soviet leaders had not directly informed them that an Egyptian attack against Israel was imminent, although for Moscow to have done so would have meant betraying its Arab clients. The criticism also assumes that the Soviets knew the precise timing of the attack in advance. A major lesson of the October War—and of the U.S.-sponsored disengagement agreements that were negotiated in its wake between Israel, on the one hand, and Egypt and Syria, on the other—was that mutual superpower "restraint" and cooperation were more difficult to effect in practice than in theory.[10]

Other reasons for the decline of the political side of detente were the Watergate scandal, which appeared to make President Nixon a little too eager to shore up his dwindling domestic fortunes by pressing ahead in relations with Moscow; North Vietnam's dramatic defeat of the South in April 1975; and Soviet (and Cuban) military assistance to Angola's Marxist guerrillas—also in 1975—which enabled the latter to assume political power in the former Portuguese colony when Lisbon retired from the scene. Collectively, these and other events contributed to the sense in the United States that Soviet diplomacy had entered a particularly active phase, marked by a greater willingness to challenge American and Western interests than in the past and to assume greater risks in the process. Political commentators in the United States began to assert that detente was the Cold War by another name, a new Kremlin tactic to achieve the same old ends, a Soviet ruse to lull the Americans into a false sense of security— Moscow's equivalent of "what's mine is mine and what's yours is negotiable."

The criticisms seemed to catch Soviet leaders off guard. Kremlin spokesmen had never sought to hide their contention that "wars of national liberation" and the "international class struggle" would proceed despite the arrival of detente between the superpowers. This was part and parcel of "peaceful coexistence." From the Soviet perspective, the worldwide advance of such "progressive" forces was a "law-governed" pattern of historical development that could not be arrested, even had Moscow and Washington attempted to do so. Throughout the 1970s, the Soviets argued that the relaxation of tensions between the two most powerful countries of the socialist and imperialist camps should not be held hostage to events in third areas, even in those regions of the world in which Moscow had become directly involved militarily, often at the perceived expense of the United States and its allies.[11]

The Soviet explanation was self-serving, of course, but not without a certain logic. In Soviet eyes, one of the consequences of rough military equivalence was what has been termed the paralytic effect of nuclear weapons. Unable to threaten one another credibly with a nuclear attack for fear of the consequences, the two superpowers could now compete as equals for political and military influence in those areas not identified by either as a vital national security interest, such as sub-Saharan Africa. When the Soviets spoke of the "historic significance" of nuclear parity, they meant in part that their military power now entitled them to assume a greater role in international political affairs—a role not substantially different from that played by the United States throughout the postwar period. Why else go to the trouble to acquire strategic nuclear forces as numerous and capable as those of the United States, civilian members of the Poliburo must have asked, if not to use them for political ends? When, in the aftermath of the October 1973 war, the United States succeeded in virtually exluding the Soviet Union from the negotiations that resulted in the separation of Israeli and Arab military forces, the Kremlin protested vigorously. As the "other" superpower, Moscow was "entitled" to take part in those discussions and to guarantee their provisions. Washington's success in preventing Soviet participation was denounced in Moscow as a blatant case of U.S. unilateralism.

Needless to say, the United States did not find the Soviet case persuasive. What the Kremlin claimed to see as a natural outgrowth of military equality, American policymakers perceived as Soviet meddling and a naked attempt to exploit U.S. reluctance to "mix it up" politically in the wake of the Vietnam War. The cumulative effect in the United States of what were regarded as Soviet abuses of American patience was encapsulated in candidate Jimmy Carter's declaration in the fall of 1976 that detente had become a one-way street. If elected, he pledged, Moscow would be held to account—implying that without a change in Soviet behavior, future cooperation on sensitive political and military questions might become impossible.

Arms Control Under Attack

The deterioration in political relations notwithstanding, detente might have survived in some truncated form after 1976 had it not been for the emergence in this country of articulate and well-organized opposition to SALT in particular and the arms control process more generally. The increasing skepticism, even hostility, toward the negotiation of limitations on U.S. and Soviet nuclear forces had several sources.

The first had to do with the rate and kind of Soviet military modernization after the signing in 1972 of the ABM Treaty and the Interim Agreement. In the first four years after SALT I, the Kremlin began the deployment of three new types of ICBMs, each equipped with multiple warheads. The largest of these missile systems, the SS-18, was armed with ten independently-targetable reentry vehicles. As a result of these deployments, the number of Soviet land-based missile warheads increased by a factor of four: from approximately 1500 in 1972 to 6000 in the early 1980s. In addition, the new weapons boasted significantly improved accuracies, leading to fears by some in the United States of a counterforce attack against American Minuteman and Titan missiles.

This development was alarming to some U.S. strategic analysts, including Paul Nitze, one of the country's leading conservative defense intellectuals and the man most responsible for the drafting in 1950 of NSC-68, the Truman administration's plan for the large-scale expansion of U.S. military forces. Dire warnings began to appear about the possibility of a Soviet nuclear strike against America's land-based missiles during an extreme crisis, the purpose of which would be to deprive the United States of its most capable weapon systems.[12] According to this scenario, the President might do nothing in response, rather than retaliate with submarine-based missiles, which, because of their lower accuracies and yields, are more suitable for strikes against population centers and "soft" military targets than such "hardened" installations as Soviet ICBM silos. To order such retaliation would be to invite a second Soviet strike against American cities. Whatever the merits of the argument (which were debatable, to say the least), it served to promote the popular impression that the Kremlin had attained a position of strategic superiority—a judgment, incidentally, not shared during this period by the U.S. Joint Chiefs of Staff.

Beginning in 1974, Moscow also initiated procurement of a new bomber aircraft, code-named "Backfire" in the West and, in 1978, deployment of a new generation of multiple-warhead submarine-launched missiles. Soviet conventional forces and theater-range ballistic missiles were also being modernized—and at a rate most Western observers found disturbing. It was during these years that a number of analyses in the U.S. media first appeared, warning of the "relentless Soviet military buildup."

A second and related source of the growing opposition to arms control centered on charges of Soviet non-compliance with existing agreements. In Agreed Interpretation J of the Interim Agreement, the two countries undertook the obligation not to increase significantly the dimensions of land-based ICBM launchers "in the process of modernization and replacement." They also agreed that "significantly" meant increases in the range of 10 to 15 percent. When the Soviets began to replace a portion of their older ICBMs with two new and substantially larger systems—the SS-17s and SS-19s—a number of American analysts cried foul. The purpose of the constraint on ICBM launchers, they protested, was to prevent Moscow from deploying significantly larger missiles, and here they were doing it anyway! They went on to argue that this constituted a violation of the spirit if not the letter of Agreed Interpretation J. The American case was weak, however, as only the missiles were from 30 to 55 percent larger than their predecessors; modifications to the silos remained within permissible limits.

There was also speculation that Moscow was secretly deploying ICBMs mounted on mobile launchers and that it was manufacturing and clandestinely storing hundreds of land-based missiles for possible use in a protracted nuclear war. While some in the United States worried about these alleged Soviet activities, there was nothing in SALT I to prohibit them. Other, more esoteric charges were leveled against the Kremlin, most of them having to do with the ABM treaty and alleged Soviet non-compliance with several of its provisions.

When the superpowers concluded SALT I, they established a body, known as the Standing Consultative Commission, to oversee implementation of the agreements. Both parties used the SCC to air their grievances and to press for full compliance whenever they believed that their negotiating partner was not fulfilling its obligations under the terms of those accords. As late as 1979 the Carter administration reported that it was satisfied, on the whole, with the Soviet record in SALT and that the SCC had performed its intended function well. Despite these assurances, the charges of Soviet "cheating" persisted and multiplied.

The Kremlin's response to the anti-SALT campaign in the United States was interesting. The Soviets not only denied that they had committed any of these alleged violations but accused American critics of arms control of seeking to sabotage detente and thus prevent the conclusion of any additional accords. Their real objective, Moscow alleged, was to pollute the political atmosphere so thoroughly as to make future superpower cooperation impossible and to lay the groundwork for the restoration of American military superiority. At the same time, the Soviets expressed guarded optimism that the "forces of realism" in the United States, by which they meant the pro-detente voices in the Nixon, Ford, and Carter administrations, would continue to hold sway and resist the temptation to succumb to such "primitive anti-Sovietism." Beginning in 1977, Kremlin leaders went one step further by renouncing any Soviet interest in the attainment of strategic superiority. Moscow was content, Brezhnev emphasized on several occasions, with the maintenance of parity and would do nothing to upset that relationship. At the same time, the Soviet leader warned that having achieved rough equality, the Kremlin would never allow the United States to regain the military advantage it had once enjoyed.

The Carter Years and SALT II

Such was the state of relations when Jimmy Carter, a centrist Democrat who had served as Georgia's governor earlier in the decade, assumed the presidency in January 1977. Carter's four years in office were marked by an acceleration of the erosion of detente that had been under way since 1974. The events surrounding that deterioration—the Kremlin's military intervention in the Horn of Africa, frictions over the president's human rights policy, U.S. recognition of the People's Republic of China, the furor over the presence of a Soviet combat brigade in Cuba, and finally, the invasion of Afghanistan—are familiar and need not be recounted in detail.

As damaging as these developments were to the fabric of detente, however, they were secondary to—and in a sense derivative of—a less evident drama being played out by the superpowers. The engine that underlay the relaxation of tensions between Washington and Moscow was arms control. Take away the good-faith effort to limit the military competition, and the struggle to improve political relations would be almost certain to founder. In the end, it was the brief coincidence in American and Soviet thinking—that each saw that the other side recognized the futility of trying to win the nuclear arms race and was therefore prepared to settle for approximate equality—that made possible not only the first SALT agreements but also the attempts to manage more effectively some of the outstanding political differences between the superpowers. Once the leaders of both countries became convinced that their counterparts were determined either to attain (in the Soviet case) or to regain (in the American case) meaningful military superiority, arms control and detente were doomed. By 1978, that conviction was already forming in Washington and Moscow.

Under these less than auspicious conditions, U.S. and Soviet arms control negotiators struggled to complete the second strategic arms limitation agreement. They succeeded, despite the deterioration in relations, and in June 1979 Carter and Brezhnev journeyed to Vienna and signed SALT II. The treaty, which had taken seven years to negotiate, ran to 19 articles and 10,000 words.[13] There was also a three-year protocol banning the deployment of mobile missile launchers and regulating cruise missile ranges, an agreed data base on the number of strategic offensive arms, and a joint statement of principles to guide future negotiations. The treaty itself was far more comprehensive than the Interim Agreement of 1972: It set equal ceilings on launchers for major strategic nuclear delivery vehicles, including long-range bombers; limited each side, in effect, to 1200 multiple-warhead missiles; and indirectly constrained the total number of nuclear weapons that could be deployed on ICBMs and SLBMs. In addition, it prohibited the two countries from procuring more than one new type of land-based missile for the duration of the agreement and elaborated new procedures for monitoring compliance. All in all, it was probably the most complex security arrangement ever negotiated by sovereign states. Unfortunately, it took extensive effort for even the educated layperson to understand.

SALT II provoked enormous controversy in this country. Groups opposed to the agreement did not wait for its signing to begin the campaign against it. The treaty was denounced in publications, lectures, and television programs as a give-away to the Russians. When the Senate initiated hearings on the accord during the summer, the opposition focused on three alleged defects. First, it was argued, the agreement made for poor arms control. Not only did the treaty fail to mandate significant reductions in missiles and warheads, it actually permitted the latter to increase. In addition, SALT II did not relieve the problem of the vulnerability of U.S. ICBMs to a Soviet nuclear strike; in fact, it would exacerbate the problem by permitting the Soviets to add several thousand high-accuracy land-based missile warheads to their arsenal. Second, doubts were expressed about the treaty's verifiability. Critics alleged that compliance with several parts of the agreement could not be monitored by the United States with high confidence; without foolproof verification, it was feared, the Soviets might cheat with impunity. And third, many Americans felt that the failure to count the Soviet Backfire bomber as a long-range weapon system (and to control it through the treaty) was an inexcusable omission, even though Brezhnev, in a separate document, pledged to limit production of the medium-range aircraft to existing levels and not to equip it with probes for in-flight refueling.

Defenders of SALT II responded that the numerical limits on strategic nuclear delivery vehicles, on MIRVed missiles, and on the "fractionation" of warheads (the placing of ever greater numbers of nuclear weapons on a single ICBM or SLBM) constituted a ceiling on many dimensions of the otherwise unlimited military competition, enabling U.S. planners to determine with some precision the future scope and character of the Soviet threat. While not perfect, these constraints were of obvious military value and could be supplemented in SALT III. They also argued that U.S. capabilities for monitoring compliance were good enough and would soon improve. Finally, SALT's champions dismissed the expressions of concern over the Backfire as misplaced, stressing that the bomber had been designed and was deployed for use against "theater" military targets in Europe and Asia; its utility as a strategic weapon system—that is, for attacks against the United States—they described as marginal.

Some critics also urged that ratification of the treaty be withheld as a form of punishment for Soviet misconduct more generally. Senators were advised to vote no on the agreement in order to express U.S. displeasure with the Kremlin's alleged violations of previous accords, its meddling in Africa, and its lack of respect for the fundamental human rights of its citizens. The politics of linkage had seldom been so explicit.

As it turned out, the day of reckoning for SALT II never arrived. The "discovery" of a Soviet combat brigade in Cuba in August 1979 temporarily diverted Congressional attention away from the treaty. By the time the administration determined that several thousand Soviet troops had been stationed in that Caribbean island since the early 1960s and that they posed no real threat to U.S. security, whatever modest momentum had been generated in support of SALT had dissipated.[14] The seizure of the American embassy in Tehran in November of that year further diminished interest in the treaty. The Soviets, perhaps convinced that the agreement was doomed anyway, delivered the coup de grace to SALT in December when they dispatched 80,000 troops to Afghanistan to prevent the collapse of the Marxist regime in Kabul. In the wake of the invasion, Carter asked the Senate to suspend consideration of the treaty. It was never again brought up for formal debate.

Eleven months later Reagan trounced Carter at the polls, in part on the strength of the Republican candidate's denunciation of detente in principle and the SALT II treaty in particular. Among other promises, Reagan pledged, once elected, to restore "a margin of military safety"—a euphemism for the reestablishment of military superiority—and to negotiate "real" arms control or none at all.

Toward an Assessment

What are we to make of detente and especially the attempt to control through formal agreement the size and capabilities of U.S. and Soviet strategic nuclear forces? Was that effort destined to fail, given the fundamentally adversarial nature of superpower relations? Was it unrealistic to imagine that Washington and Moscow could to a degree coordinate their actions in what is manifestly the most sensitive issue area for sovereign countries: the safeguarding of their national security? Did the two sides in a sense not aim high enough, settling for a regulated arms race when they should have been concentrating on actual disarmament? And what about the political dimension of detente? Could either superpower for long have put aside the pursuit of unilateral advantage in the name of cooperation and mutual restraint?

The SALT Legacy

It has been a basic proposition of this book that American and Soviet interests are essentially competitive and that as such superpower cooperation is the exception rather than the rule. For Washington and Moscow to overcome the urge to compete requires that they have a clear incentive to do so. Only if they perceive mutual advantage will the two superpowers sometimes seek to coordinate policy and be willing to subordinate immediate notions of gain to a larger objective from which each believes it will derive some greater good. Countries do not act out of a sense of altruism; with very few exceptions, national leaders act to secure on behalf of the state some benefit or advantage.

To the extent that negotiated arms control promised to produce an outcome that from the self-interested perspective of the two parties would be preferable to that which could be obtained through unilateral action, the United States and the Soviet Union were prepared to make the effort. Political scientists employ the term regime to account for those instances in which states cooperate when their more typical response would be to compete. A security regime, meaning cooperation on military-related issues, is defined as "those principles, rules, and norms that permit nations to be restrained in their behavior in the belief that others will reciprocate." It is, the definition continues, "more than the following of short-run self-interest."[15]

Is it appropriate to characterize the SALT process between 1969 and 1979 as a regime? With suitable caveats, the answer is yes.

A t the most elemental level, what made the negotiation of strategic arms control both possible and desirable was the recognition on both sides, however brief and reluctant, that the attainment of a position of usable nuclear superiority was an illusion. Fueling that realization was the fact that neither country possessed or believed it possible to achieve the capacity to shield itself—should it ever strike its adversary first—from a crippling retaliatory blow. In addition, each seemed to understand that, for the time being at least, even the attempt to defend itself against nuclear attack through the procurement of anti-ballistic missile systems could accelerate the nuclear competition and in the end leave both countries worse off than before. No altruism there. Had either antagonist believed in 1969 that it could have obtained an important military advantage—such as the ability to limit damage to its population and industry—through the acquisition of more and better weapons, the SALT negotiations would in all likelihood never have convened.

To argue that the Soviet Union began the process in order to constrain U.S. military programs while leaving itself a free hand is to overstate the obvious—namely, that each party to a negotiation seeks the most advantageous outcome. Doubtless, the United States did the same. To move from that observation to the conclusion that Moscow succeeded in that game is to suggest that American political leaders were either dimwitted or weak-willed. The more refined version of the allegation is that the United States struck the best deal available to it at the time, recognizing that the Soviet strategic buildup was in full swing while the number of U.S. strategic forces (excluding warheads) had stabilized in 1967. Better to place some limits on Soviet capabilities by concluding a partial agreement than to take no action at all. There is an element of truth to this second charge but its significance is often exaggerated.

The Nixon administration decided in 1972 that an agreement formalizing the principle of rough nuclear equality, while also prohibiting certain kinds of military procurements and deployments, was in the national security interest of the United States. Facilitating that decision was the implicit recognition that marginal advantages in terms of missiles, bombers, or warheads were of little military value one way or the other, given the robustness of each country's retaliatory forces and the adversary's persistent vulnerability to such retaliation.

The more salient critique of SALT I is that it did not go far enough, that there were important aspects to the military competition that were inadequately controlled or left unregulated altogether. The Soviet Union's deployment of three new types of ICBMs (larger and more capable than the systems they replaced) in the period after the conclusion of the Interim Agreement is a case in point, as was the failure of the two sides to ban or at least limit the deployment of MIRV warheads. The inability to prevent these "improvements" in weaponry diminished the utility of the agreement as a whole and gave rise to the impression that the Soviet Union had somehow profited from SALT I more than the United States. That argument is not without merit, although under the provisions of the accord Washington was entitled to undertake comparable actions in defense of its national security, had already done so, and was continuing in those efforts. The problem was timing. The Kremlin's program to "modernize" its nuclear forces was ongoing and broadly gauged; the American program had peaked five years earlier, was more modest, at least initially, and also more selective.

As suggested earlier, the blow from which arms control never recovered was the growing sense, evident first in the United States, that the other side had never really abandoned the quest for military superiority and was employing the cover of SALT to assist in the realization of that objective. It was in this context that charges of Soviet cheating became significant. It was not so much that Moscow might not be keeping its word, although that would be unfortunate; rather, it was that the Soviets might be circumventing the agreements purposefully, in order to advantage themselves militarily. At some point in time, these activities, together with those not prohibited by SALT, might translate into a military posture that would enable the Soviet Union to prevail over the United States in the event of war. Such was the fear, at least, of those who made this case.

By the end of the Carter administration, Soviet authorities had taken up the same theme in reverse: that while paying lip service to arms control, the United States had every intention of regaining the initiative in the arms race and in reestablishing its former military preeminence. In support of its contention, the Kremlin pointed an accusing finger at such weapons programs as the MX ICBM, 200 of which were to be deployed in the Great Basin of Nevada and Utah, the high-accuracy Trident II SLBM, which was to begin testing toward the end of the 1980s, the Pershing II intermediate-range missile, slated for deployment in Germany, and the planned procurement of thousands of air-, ground-, and sea-launched cruise missiles.

Because SALT II permitted the building of all these weapons, as well as many others, defending the pursuit of arms control by underscoring the value of the treaty in restraining the strategic competition lacked resonance. Moreover, neither government demonstrated much confidence in that argument. The Carter administration based its appeal for ratification of SALT II on the less-than-stirring contention that the treaty was a "modestly useful" device to constrain certain Soviet military activities and that it was preferable to no agreement at all. The Kremlin emphasized that SALT II was a necessary precondition to the achievement of more substantial reductions and controls during the next phase. The very real limitations that were contained in the agreement got lost in the noise.

Ultimately, how one assesses the SALT experiment and particularly the collapse of the process at the end of the 1970s turns on one's estimate of what is realistic to expect of such rivals. Did either side harbor secret plans to upset the strategic equilibrium that lay at the heart of the process and thereby hope to seize for itself a position of military superiority? It is impossible to answer that question definitively without access to all the relevant documents and without the administration of truth serum to each senior government official on both sides. But the evidence at hand does permit some informed judgments.

We know, for example, that the Nixon administration entered the SALT negotiations with the apparent conviction that nuclear superiority could not be maintained and that a posture of "strategic sufficiency" and "essential equivalence" was adequate for purposes of deterrence. Whether the Soviet leadership reached the same or a similar conclusion is impossible to determine. In addition, the two sides undertook the obligation, expressed in the preamble of the ABM treaty, to "achieve at the earliest possible date the cessation of the nuclear arms race and to take effective measures toward reductions in strategic arms. . . ." More to the point, in concluding that agreement, the two countries foreswore the single most promising avenue to limit the extent of damage should a nuclear war erupt between them—namely, the option of nationwide ABM defenses. By so doing, they affirmed the fact that mutual societal vulnerability underlay their deterrent relationship. In other words, in light of the technical realities existing at the time, neither could hope to "win" a major war fought with nuclear weapons.

On the negative side of the ledger, both persisted in the development of new and more capable strategic offensive weapons, including those with the requisite accuracies to target and destroy such fixed military installations as missile silos and command-and-control facilities. With enough counterforce weapons, one side might be emboldened to strike first in a crisis in the belief that by eliminating some percentage of the opponent's retaliatory forces on the ground or (in the case of submarines) in port, the effect of the adversary's inevitable counterblow might be mitigated. This is one, though hardly the only, explanation for the Soviet Union's investment in a new generation of multiple-warhead ICBMs after the signing of SALT I in 1972 and for the American interest in both the MX and Trident II missiles.

Surely, however, Washington and Moscow also understood (and said repeatedly) that as powerful and as accurate as these advanced weapons were, they could not destroy more than a fraction of the other side's total nuclear arsenal, leaving many thousands of weapons for a retaliatory strike.

The unavoidable conclusion is that both superpowers undertook military programs that each regarded as a prudent hedge against the failure of deterrence but which the other interpreted as evidence of at least a lingering or implicit interest in strategic superiority. Once revealed, these actions generated pressure on decisionmakers in each capital to keep pace and to demonstrate equal resolve, setting off what was characterized in an earlier chapter as an echo effect. The result was a gradual loss of confidence on each side that its negotiating partner was bargaining in good faith. By 1980, this echo had become so intense as to reduce the perceived utility of what had been achieved and to make highly problematic any new efforts at controlling the arms competition.

Two other points should be made in assessing the contribution of superpower arms control to reducing the likelihood of war and limiting various aspects of the U.S.-Soviet military competition. Supplementing the more visible negotiations on strategic weapons, Washington and Moscow quietly concluded two agreements in 1971—the first on upgrading the Hotline and the second on measures to guard against the outbreak of accidental or inadvertent nuclear war—which are in force today. Each is a continuing reminder that for all their differences the two countries are enormously sensitive to the dangers posed by nuclear weapons and share a common interest in preventing their use.

The second point is that despite the abuse that the United States and the Soviet Union have heaped on one another regarding each other's alleged non-compliance with both SALT I and SALT II, as of late 1986 both have been content for the most part to abide by the terms of those accords—although this may be changing—offering strong circumstantial evidence in support of the proposition that whatever their private misgivings and public postures, the two governments perceive the ABM treaty, the Interim Agreement, and SALT II to be of some value in buttressing deterrence and in restraining the military activities and programs of the other side. This issue is considered in greater detail in Chapter 6.

The Political Aspects of Detente

Evaluating the political component of detente is even more elusive than reviewing arms control, if for no other reason than because the results of the former are more difficult to quantify. What is the standard against which to measure progress? What were U.S. and Soviet expectations? To what extent was the relaxation of political tensions dependent on success in controlling the military rivalry? Or was it the improvement of relations at the political level that opened the way for and made possible the first steps in arms control?

To a degree, political detente and progress in arms control went hand in hand. During the first few years of the Nixon administration in particular, relations between Washington and Moscow improved across a broad front. Both sides seemed equally determined to navigate the transition from the Cold War to a kind of regulated competition. It is true, nonetheless, that the SALT talks became the very symbol of the new relationship. It was no accident, therefore, that when those negotiations yielded tangible products in the form of the ABM treaty and the Interim Agreement, the outlook for the further positive development of political relations also seemed quite favorable. Predictably enough, when SALT turned sour later in the decade, the number of political problems between the superpowers multiplied.

The connection between the military and political aspects of detente operated on at least two levels. First, the ability of the two countries to negotiate successfully on the control of nuclear weapons—traditionally the most sensitive and difficult issue dividing them—gave each the confidence to extend the effort at accommodation to other areas. The containment of their political rivalry might have appeared less daunting than at any previous juncture. This is one way, for example, to explain the willingness of Nixon and Brezhnev to affix their signatures to the Basic Principles of Relations agreement at the first Moscow summit. Both may have believed sincerely that an invisible threshold had been crossed and that the relationship had matured sufficiently to permit the elaboration of certain agreed "rules of the road." The difficulty, of course, was that the accord operated at such a level of generality that it lacked effective content. Among its several shortcomings, the agreement left to each side the determination of what constituted restraint in the conduct of its diplomacy, making it all too easy for the United States to accuse the Soviet Union of seeking unilateral advantage and vice versa. The attempts to supplement these general principles with more precise and focused norms and procedures never got very far.

A t a second level, the effort to generalize the SALT experience had a decidedly negative impact on the development of better political relations between the superpowers because each side misapplied the lessons. Arms control was a "success" because for one relatively brief moment the interests of the United States and the Soviet Union in averting a new, costly, and destabilizing round in the military competition converged. Moreover, by agreeing not to undertake certain weapons programs and to curtail various activities already under way in exchange for similar concessions on the other side, each could prevent the possible deterioration of its military position. The incentives to cooperate were stronger than the incentives to defect, to use the term preferred by political scientists.

Contrast this to the political situation. Neither Washington nor Moscow had any overarching reason to believe in 1972 that the costs of competing for power and influence in the world would exceed the benefits. In fact, Soviet leaders, in particular, perceived the reverse to be the case: that the codification of nuclear parity meant that the Kremlin was far more capable than in the past of challenging Western interests in those areas not identified by the "imperialist camp" as vital to its security. Within implicit but mutually recognized limits, Moscow seemed to believe, the risks of competing with the United States were manageable and the potential payoffs significant. Eventually, the Carter administration did seek to attach a price to the Kremlin's higher international political profile by threatening to link Soviet restraint to the conclusion of follow-up arms control agreements—a linkage that Soviet leaders rejected and claimed not to understand. In the end, the United States retreated from that position and the second strategic arms agreement was concluded.

It was a mistake, in other words, for American and Soviet leaders to assume (to the extent that they did so) that the same factors which induced them to place some limits on the nuclear arms race would also assist in the regulation of the political competition. The obvious mutuality of interest in military detente had no direct counterpart in other dimensions of the relationship. This is not to suggest that greater progress in managing the political component of detente could not have been achieved with additional efforts, only that the process was in no sense automatic. Success in arms control was a necessary but insufficient precondition for a sustained improvement in U.S.-Soviet relations.

Could the collapse of U.S.-Soviet detente at the end of the 1970s have been prevented or was its decline in some sense inevitable? Had the leaderships in both countries retained their confidence in the essence of the SALT bargain—they won't seek nuclear superiority if we don't—the abject failure to contain the political competition might not have proved fatal to the overall process of accommodation. Critical in this regard was the highly visible character of the Kremlin's weapons modernization programs after 1972, which, in American eyes, cast doubt on the Soviet Union's willingness to settle for parity in military potential.

This in turn led detente's critics in the United States to discern a connection between what they saw as Moscow's emerging nuclear advantage and its new-found willingness to intervene either directly or through the use of surrogate forces in such Third World conflicts as the Angolan civil war and Ethiopia's conflict with Somalia. It was soon thereafter that U.S. defense appropriations began to increase, detente became synonymous with weakness in debates over American foreign policy, and it was Moscow's turn to play the jilted suitor. By this time predisposed to cast the actions of the other side in the least favorable light, Washington and Moscow gradually came to embrace the idea that a lasting relaxation of tensions was a chimera. The "inevitable" decline of detente became a self-fulfilling prophecy.

Bird of Peace, Bird of War / *Mike Quon*

6 The Reagan Difference 1981–1985

The transition from one U.S. administration to the next has always brought with it changes in policy, some dramatic and some less so. When Eisenhower succeeded Truman in 1953, the first Republican president since Hoover promised greater fiscal austerity in government, a more assertive American posture in world affairs, and a New Look in defense. Eight years later, Kennedy came to office vowing to "get America moving again" by awakening the country from what some critics had termed its economic and social somnolence.

Yet, in retrospect, what strikes the observer are not so much the *departures* but the fundamental *continuities* in postwar U.S. policies. For the most part, American leaders have been content to amend, revise, and fine-tune the work of their predecessors; those with loftier goals have been compelled to seek the enactment of their initiatives incrementally, content to settle for much less than what they had in mind at the outset.

The election of Ronald Reagan in 1980 constituted something of a break with that tradition. In many respects it represented the first real sea change in U.S. politics since 1945, signaling a sharp turn to the right. Most will agree that the "Reagan Revolution" has had a profound impact on many aspects of American life. And nowhere has that impact been greater than in those dimensions of government policy—foreign affairs, defense, and arms control—that comprise the focus of this book.

Since the late 1950s the U.S. government had identified the easing of political tensions with the Soviet Union and the limitation of nuclear weapons as important objectives. The many downturns in superpower relations notwithstanding, the commitment to achieve some progress along each of those dimensions remained at the core of American diplomacy through six administrations, reaching its most developed expression during the eight years of Presidents Nixon and Ford. Reagan, by contrast, had denounced both SALT and much of U.S. policy toward the Soviet Union during the course of the 1980 campaign, strongly suggesting that in the event of his election he would abandon the former and transform the latter.

The Reagan critique of detente and arms control, shared by most of the new president's national security advisers, was built around three main propositions:

- *First*, that the very notion of a stable, mutually advantageous relationship with the U.S.S.R. was a contradiction in terms, owing to the anti-democratic nature of the Soviet system and the Kremlin's aggressive and expansionist foreign policy. The comparison to Hitler's Germany was made often and explicitly. As a "totalitarian" regime, the Soviet Union could not be dealt with on the same bases on which the United States conducted its relations with other countries, be they allies or adversaries. The way to deal with an international bully, in other words, was not to appease but to resist and to do so on a global scale.

- *Second*, that arms control, as symbolized by the SALT process, had been a fraud. Far from reducing the number of nuclear weapons, the critics alleged, the 1972 Interim Agreement had actually permitted both sides to increase their weapons holdings and to deploy new and more deadly missile systems. SALT II, according to Reagan, was no better. Worse yet, under the guise of arms control, Moscow had attained a position of military superiority that Soviet leaders had begun to translate at Western expense into greater international political influence.

- *Third*, and the most controversial, that the loss of American military preeminence was not inevitable, as detente's advocates implied. This trend, it was argued, could be reversed, given renewed political will and devotion of adequate resources. While vague on how that goal might be attained, what precisely might be required, and how long it might take, the Reagan commitment to the restoration of a military "margin of safety" was unmistakable.

Kremlin leaders must have listened with great interest to both the content and the tenor of the American debate over detente and nuclear arms control. At stake for Brezhnev was nothing less than the central thrust of his foreign policy line: that despite the persistence of strong anti-Soviet elements in the United States, the Kremlin could do business with Washington as long as Republican and Democratic "realists"—those who understood that objective conditions (i.e., the arrival of nuclear parity) left no alternative to the pursuit of normalized relations—continued to direct U.S. policy. As late as February 1981, Brezhnev was affirming the Soviet commitment to the relaxation of international tensions and to negotiated arms control, despite the dramatic deterioration in superpower relations over the previous two years and the election in the United States three months before of detente's severest critic. The Soviets may have believed that, once in office, Reagan would jettison much of his campaign rhetoric, move to the political center, and become, in essence, a second Nixon in the conduct of foreign policy. If so, they were soon disappointed.

That realization did not burst upon Soviet leaders fully formed. It would take several years for the Kremlin to conclude that the administration's rejection of detente was unequivocal, and that its determination to restore American military power was far more than campaign windowdressing. The content of Soviet policy toward the United States changed slowly. As the Kremlin moved to embrace the view that the Reagan challenge was indeed fundamental, the issue for the leadership became how best to respond, both politically and militarily.

Even during the best of times, governments do not find such decisions simple or easy; in the Soviet case the political uncertainties generated by the advanced ages and ill health of the country's senior leaders made them especially difficult. Between November 1982 and March 1985, three General Secretaries of the Soviet Communist Party—Leonid Brezhnev, Yuri Andropov, and Konstantin Chernenko—were to die in office. It was only with the elevation of Mikhail Gorbachev that the Soviet Union could at last look forward to a period of renewed political vigor and stability.

If U.S.-Soviet relations between 1981 and 1985 had about them a certain *déjà vu* quality, there was good reason. On both sides, it seems, the predominant images were those of hostility, conflict, and great danger—essentially the same set of images that dominated American and Soviet views of the superpower competition from the late 1940s to the late 1960s. While the sources of tension were many and diverse, the revival of the conviction on the part of each government that its principal adversary had settled on a course aimed at nothing less than the attainment of military superiority played a central role. It is hardly a coincidence that similar fears fueled and sustained the Cold War.

It is well to remember that what had enabled the partial progress in controlling the arms race during the 1970s was the shared conviction that neither country could hope to maintain a position of meaningful military advantage and that the limitation of U.S. and Soviet strategic nuclear forces was therefore both possible and desirable. By the time of the 1980 presidential election, that understanding had been called into question, explicitly in the United States and, we can assume, implicitly in the Soviet Union. During its first four years, the Reagan administration spent roughly a trillion dollars to expand and upgrade U.S. military capabilities in the apparent belief that such expenditures were necessary both to prevent the outbreak of nuclear war and to deter Soviet "adventurism." The administration also justified its military buildup by underscoring the need to bargain with the Soviet Union from a position of strength in the event of any future arms control negotiations. By the end of Reagan's first term, however, this strategy of "build up to build down" had failed to produce any new agreements to limit or reduce nuclear weapons.

As a consequence of these and related developments, by the mid-1980s the two superpowers found themselves not only at political loggerheads but poised on the brink of a qualitatively new round of the arms competition that neither could afford and from which neither was likely to profit militarily.

Setting the Tone

At his first presidential press conference, on January 29, 1981, Reagan was asked to clarify his position regarding the SALT II treaty and to share with the American public his views on the long-range intentions of the Soviet Union. His responses were illuminating, for they provided an early clue to the likely direction of administration policy concerning arms control and relations with Moscow. On SALT, the president reiterated his opposition to Senate ratification, arguing, "I don't think that a treaty—SALT means strategic arms limitation—that actually permits a buildup, on both sides, of strategic nuclear weapons can properly be called that." He also condemned the agreement on the grounds that it would authorize an "immediate increase" in Soviet ballistic missile warheads and that it provided no reliable mechanism to monitor the number of warheads deployed on a given Soviet missile system.[1]

On the question of Soviet intentions, the president's remarks were equally pointed, revealing not only his deep suspicion of Kremlin motives but also his visceral dislike of detente. "So far," Reagan began, "detente's been a one-way street that the Soviet Union has used to pursue its own aims." He went on to say,

> I know of no leader of the Soviet Union since the revolution, and including the present leadership, who has not more than once repeated in the various Communist congresses they hold their determination that their goal must be the promotion of world revolution and a one-world Socialist or Communist state. . . .
>
> Now as long as they do that and as long as they, at the same time, have openly and publicly declared that the only morality they recognize is what will further their cause—meaning they reserve unto themselves the right to commit any crime, to lie, to cheat, in order to attain that, and that is moral, not immoral, and we operate on a different set of standards—I think, when you do business with them . . . you keep that in mind.[2]

What made Reagan's comments remarkable was not that he held such views—millions of Americans felt and continue to feel much the same way—but his willingness as president to render his sentiments explicit in a public forum. It marked the beginning of a pattern that was to endure.

Moscow reacted sharply to this and later presidential pronouncements in which Reagan equated Soviet behavior with various forms of criminal activity, complaining that the new administration had elevated anti-Communism to "state policy." The Kremlin also responded in kind. In 1983, one senior Soviet analyst not prone to name-calling described certain unnamed U.S. government officials as "thick-headed," "loudmouth" provincials.[3]

The war of words between Washington and Moscow escalated during the president's first two years in office. In an address to the British Parliament on June 8, 1982, for example, Reagan took dead aim at the Soviet system, using the word "decay" to characterize its essential condition. He went on to express his confidence that the "renewed strength of the democratic movement, complemented by a global campaign for freedom" would eventually sweep Marxism-Leninism aside, relegating it to the "ash heap of history."[4] The president's anti-Soviet rhetoric reached a crescendo of sorts in March 1983, during a speech to the National Association of Evangelicals in Orlando, Florida. In the course of his remarks, Reagan denounced the Soviet Union in the most vivid of terms as the "focus of evil in the modern world," warning against "simple-minded appeasement or wishful thinking about our adversaries." Returning to what had become by this time one his of favorite themes, he concluded by underscoring his faith in the staying power of the democratic ideal. "I believe," the president declared,

> that Communism is another sad, bizarre chapter in human history whose last pages even now are being written. I believe this because the source of our strength in the quest for human freedom is not material but spiritual, and because it knows no limitation, it must terrify and and ultimately triumph over those who would enslave their fellow man.[5]

Beyond the perceived need on the part of his political advisers to buttress the president's conservative credentials on the home front, Reagan's repeated and pointed verbal assaults against the Kremlin and its ideology served the critical function of demarking the administration's Soviet policy from that which had come before, most notably the turbulent four years associated with Jimmy Carter's tenure in the White House.

In a 1977 speech at the University of Notre Dame, Carter had warned against what he termed an inordinate fear of Communism, making the point that America's fixation with the Soviet Union and Marxism-Leninism had distorted in some fundamental sense both the formulation and the conduct of U.S. foreign policy throughout the post-war period.[6] Reagan was arguing precisely the opposite: that it was the Kremlin with its commitment to the establishment of a one-world Socialist state which posed the principal and continuing threat to American interests and Western political values. The Carter administration, especially during its first two years, sought to play down the ideological dimension of the competition, to move beyond the image of two great systems in perpetual conflict, and to highlight possible areas of agreement between Washington and Moscow. The Reagan administration saw the "war of ideas" as an integral part of the relationship, did all it could to focus and sharpen that imagery, and dismissed the search for accommodation as naive. A more dramatic contrast in perspective would be difficult to imagine.

The Nuclear Buildup

The president's rhetorical skills were of obvious value to the administration in generating domestic political support for its foreign and defense policies. But images, however evocative, are no substitute for action. As Reagan pressed his case against the Kremlin, senior Pentagon officials began the time-consuming task of convincing Congress and the American public of the need to rebuild the country's defenses. They did so by painting a particularly bleak picture of U.S. military capabilities; the deficiencies could only be corrected, they asserted, through large increases in defense appropriations sustained over the better part of a decade. Both the president and Secretary of Defense Caspar Weinberger made repeated references in 1981 and 1982 to what they described as Moscow's attainment of "strategic superiority" and to the dramatic erosion of America's military position since the late 1960s. The strategy yielded impressive dividends. For fiscal year 1982, Congress approved a defense budget almost 12 percent larger than the previous year's appropriation; smaller though sizeable increases were voted in each of the three succeeding fiscal years.

In October 1981, the administration unveiled its five-year, $180 billion program to modernize U.S. strategic forces. Among its several provisions, the plan called for increased spending for continental air defenses against bombers and for improvements in strategic command, control, and communications facilities. It also urged accelerated procurement of the Trident II submarine-launched ballistic missile and the restoration of funds for the B-1 bomber program, which the Carter administration had canceled in 1977 in favor of a program to equip B-52 aircraft with long-range air-launched cruise missiles. More controversially, the Defense Department, with White House support, proposed that 100 MX intercontinental-range ballistic missiles be deployed in reconfigured Minuteman silos, pending the selection of a permanent basing mode that would afford the missiles greater protection against nuclear attack.

For the most part, Congress acceded to the administration's requests. Opposition did develop, however, to the Pentagon's plans for the MX. During the 1980 campaign, Reagan had come out against a Carter administration proposal to base the new ICBM in so-called multiple-protective shelters (or MPS), to be located in southern Nevada and southwestern Utah. MPS was a complex and expensive scheme to reduce the vulnerability of the MX to a Soviet first strike by providing the system a degree of mobility. It was also extremely unpopular with many of the people in the region, including Republican Senator Paul Laxalt of Nevada, a close adviser to candidate Reagan. Once in office, the new administration's defense officials struggled to devise an alternative basing mode that would provide the missile with a modicum of "survivability" against a preemptive attack. They failed in that effort and in frustration proposed, as an interim measure, the immediate deployment of the weapon in existing silos.

A majority in Congress took strong exception to that plan. Why deploy the country's newest intercontinental-range, land based missile in stationary installations that were already sitting ducks for Soviet weapons? Two Soviet warheads accurately placed, critics warned, could destroy one silo-based MX, each armed with 10 reentry vehicles. Theoretically, 200 Soviet weapons could wipe out the entire force. The House and Senate ordered the administration to scrap the plan for silo basing and to submit a new proposal to safeguard the system's "survivability." The battle did not end there, however, and for the next three years Congress and the Executive Branch wrestled with the issue, before concluding, reluctantly, that there was no better way to base the missile at an acceptable cost. In 1985, the two sides compromised and Congress authorized the deployment of 50 MX in silos.

On balance, however, the Reagan administration encountered little real opposition to its military programs. While some in Congress and many defense-oriented public interest groups argued that the U.S. strategic posture was not in dire need of a major overhaul and that a smaller increase in defense appropriations—on the order of 3 percent a year—would be more than adequate to meet the country's military requirements, the popular mood during the president's first eighteen months in office was to spend first and ask questions later. The dominant perception within both the Executive Branch and the Congress was one of pervasive American military weakness. That conviction, a virtual article of faith among conservative legislators and administration officials, made superfluous the kind of careful and exhaustive documentation one would have anticipated in light of the fiscal implications of the Pentagon's defense plans.

The Evolution of Nuclear Strategy

While obviously central to the administration, the strategic modernization program was only one element in a much more broadly gauged effort to restore a military margin of safety. A second and less visible dimension concerned possible revisions in military strategy. What should be the objectives of the United States in the event of a nuclear or conventional war with the Soviet Union and its allies? To what extent should existing objectives be revised? Would the forces-in-being and those slated for procurement be sufficient to accomplish American military goals?

We know from the annual reports of the Secretary of Defense that the overarching goal of U.S. military strategy has been and continues to be the deterrence of nuclear war. But what does it take to deter? Since the mid-1960s, the answer to that question had always been that the most reliable way to forestall a Soviet nuclear attack against the United States and its allies was to have the capability to frustrate the Kremlin's war aims by denying it the fruits of victory. The key to such a strategy was to have sufficient nuclear retaliatory forces to inflict on the Soviet Union a level of destruction adequate to reduce the U.S.S.R. to a heap of smoking rubble. In other words, to make certain that the *cost* to the Kremlin of going to war would exceed any anticipated *gain*. Implicit in this formula was the assumption that neither side could hope to win a large-scale nuclear exchange, given the inability to defend either the American or the Soviet population against attack.

One area in which opinions differed from administration to administration concerned targeting: What, precisely, was the United States to attack in the event that a nuclear war were to erupt between the superpowers? Between 1969 and 1981, the emphasis in U.S. strategy shifted. While retaining the capability to destroy Soviet industrial facilities and population centers, more attention was devoted to the destruction during wartime of the Kremlin's military forces—although it was less than clear to those outside official channels which forces were being targeted and how many. At no point after the early 1960s, however, were U.S. nuclear forces judged sufficient in number to execute a disarming first strike. During the Carter administration equal priority was accorded to the targeting of the Soviet Union's civilian and military leadership in the apparent belief that senior Kremlin officials, faced with the prospect of a complete breakdown in the command and control of Soviet armed forces, would resist the temptation to attack the United States even in the most extreme of crisis situations.

A second area of controversy was how most effectively to deter not an all-out, bolt-out-of-the-blue Soviet nuclear strike, which was deemed a remote possibility, but a more limited attack against discrete "target sets" in the United States or Western Europe. To meet that perceived threat, Secretary of Defense James Schlesinger in 1974 had submitted a plan to provide the president with a wider range of nuclear options than had existed in the past, affording the commander-in-chief greater flexibility in the selection of targets, both in number and in kind. The Schlesinger revision of U.S. strategy was implemented over the course of the next several years and preserved in amended form by his immediate successors.

To a significant degree, the Reagan administration's nuclear strategy, as articulated by senior Pentagon officials in testimony before Congress, was consistent with Defense Department policy from previous administrations. In his 1984 report to Congress, for example, Secretary Weinberger described the policy of deterrence in the following terms:

> We, for our part, are under no illusions about the dangers of a nuclear war between the major powers; we believe that neither side could win such a war. But this recognition on *our* part is not sufficient to prevent the outbreak of nuclear war; it is essential that the Soviet leadership understand this as well. We must make sure that the Soviet leadership, in calculating the risks of aggression, recognizes that because of our retaliatory capability, there can be no circumstances in

> which it could benefit by beginning a nuclear war at
> any level or of any duration [emphasis in the original].[7]

In the same document, Weinberger emphasized the defensive nature of U.S. strategy, arguing that the United States would never initiate a war or launch a preemptive strike against the forces or territories of other countries.

There was, however, one very important departure from previous defense policy. In his 1984 report to Congress, Weinberger was sharply critical of what most American defense analysts had come to regard as the bedrock of deterrence, namely this country's assured destruction capability. "We disagree," Weinberger declared, "with those who hold that deterrence should be based on nuclear weapons designed to destroy cities rather than military targets. Deliberately designing weapons aimed at populations is neither necessary nor sufficient for deterrence."[8] What, then, should the United States target? The Secretary was not explicit on this issue, although he did underscore the advantages of a "viable warfighting defense" that was "in being and maintained at the ready."

More to the point, Weinberger also stated that one of the three guiding principles of U.S. strategy was to terminate hostilities "at the lowest possible level of damage to the United States and its allies" and to "restore peace on favorable terms."[9] In the context of a nuclear war involving the widespread use of ballistic missiles, there are two— and only two—ways that combatants can seek both to limit damage and to restore peace under favorable conditions: To have in place effective strategic defense capabilities, including a nationwide anti-ballistic missile system, or to destroy the enemy's offensive nuclear forces in a preemptive strike—in other words, to disarm him. The most reliable means to achieve this objective would be to have some combination of *both* capabilities.

Were the objective simply to limit damage, the prompt termination of the fighting before the transition to an all-out nuclear exchange could bring that goal within reach for both sides, requiring neither reliable strategic defenses nor a disarming first strike. On the other hand, to obtain a favorable outcome in the context of a nuclear war means to prevail in some sense, an end which can be attained only by having the capacity to defend the state in a virtually leak-proof manner, by striking first, or by doing both.

Weinberger did not elaborate further on this point in his 1984 report to Congress. In later appearances before Congress and in subsequent annual reports, the Defense Secretary denied, in fact, that it had ever been his—or the president's— intention to suggest that a nuclear war between the superpowers could ever be won. In 1983, however, he seemed to believe otherwise.

Before dismissing this departure in policy as a careless oversight, it is well to remember that in the adminstration's 1981 plan to modernize U.S. strategic forces, the Defense Department attached particular importance to the deployment of the MX and to the accelerated procurement of the Trident II submarine-launched missile, either of which was expected to be accurate enough to destroy, according to the Pentagon, "the full spectrum of Soviet military targets." By the mid-1990s, the United States could have as many as 4000 high-accuracy ballistic missile warheads targeted against Soviet ICBM silos, staging areas for mobile missile systems, submarines in port, and military command and control facilities—enough to eliminate in a preemptive strike as much as 75 percent of the Kremlin's entire nuclear arsenal, assuming that Soviet nuclear forces would not be launched as American weapons were on their way.

This is not to suggest that in their determination to acquire such capabilities administration officials were seeking to implement a secret master plan that would enable them at some future point in time to attack the Soviet Union at will. The uncertainties associated with any preemptive strike—the likelihood that some significant fraction of the opponent's nuclear forces would survive and be launched in retaliation, or that the targeted missile silos might be empty by the time the enemy's forces arrive—make a surprise, bolt-out-of-the-blue nuclear attack the riskiest of military ventures. Pentagon officials could be taken at their word that their central purpose was to *buttress* deterrence, not *undermine* it, by providing the Soviet Union with the strongest of incentives never to strike first: that while both sides would absorb enormous damage in the course of a nuclear war, the Kremlin would sustain greater losses, especially in terms of its ability to conduct military operations and to retain control of its population.

The Pentagon's rationale notwithstanding, the explicit endorsement in U.S. declaratory policy in 1983 of a deterrent posture based on the twin goals of limiting damage and the termination of nuclear hostilities on terms favorable to the United States constituted one of the most significant revisions to American nuclear strategy since Mc-Namara's abandonment of the "no-cities" doctrine in the early 1960s.

The Soviets React

The change was not welcomed in all quarters. Many people, including a number of prominent defense analysts and much of the U.S. arms control community, found the administration's apparent flirtation with a nuclear war-fighting strategy profoundly troubling. Some West European authorities evidenced special anxiety. Would the shift in strategy raise or lower the nuclear threshold? Would it make war more or less likely? And how would the Soviet Union respond?

Soviet officials reacted with expressions of outrage mixed with disbelief. On the one hand, the Kremlin condemned the strategic modernization program (and later the new version of U.S. deterrence doctrine) as clear evidence of the administration's commitment to the achievement of military superiority. Twice during this period, for example, in July 1981 and then again a year later, Soviet Defense Minister Dmitry Ustinov issued dark warnings about U.S. military intentions. The objective of the American defense buildup, Ustinov alleged in 1982, was the attainment of the capability "to deliver a first strike at the Soviet Union where and when Washington finds it expedient in its reckoning that a retaliatory blow at the United States will be of less strength than under other conditions."[10]

On the other hand, Ustinov and other prominent Soviet military leaders seemed almost contemptuous of what they saw as the American effort to reestablish a position of strategic preeminence. Under no conditions, the Defense Minster asserted, could the United States hope to execute a disarming first strike against the Soviet Union in light of the "high combat readiness" of the country's strategic nuclear forces—a thinly veiled reference to the Kremlin's ability to launch its forces while under attack. Washington should not, Ustinov continued, "hypnotize itself with the possibility of achieving military superiority over the U.S.S.R. Nothing will come of that."[11]

At the same time, at least some Soviet observers must have taken note of the implicit irony of the situation: Here was the most conservative American administration in 50 years, vociferous in its denunciation of all things Soviet, endorsing elements of the Kremlin's military strategy, including the pursuit of a "damage-limiting" posture based on the targeting of the adversary's military forces (see Chapter 2).

What the Kremlin had come to regard by 1982 as a serious American bid for military superiority came at a particularly bad time for the country's leadership. Leonid Brezhnev, who had celebrated his seventy-fifth birthday in December 1981, was in failing health and had relinquished much of the day-to-day responsibility for the management of the country's political affairs to his seventy-year-old deputy, Konstantin Chernenko—an undistinguished party bureaucrat only slightly more vigorous than his patron. Two weeks after addressing an extraordinary gathering of senior Soviet military officials in late October 1982, Brezhnev was dead. KGB chief Yuri Andropov succeeded him, but at sixty-eight, his tenure in office was unlikely to be lengthy; rumors circulated in Moscow that he suffered from a combination of debilitating heart and kidney ailments that cut into his work time.

Leadership changes in the Soviet Union are often accompanied by a greater willingness on the part of the country's most powerful authorities to tolerate debate on important policy issues. To be sure, such debates take place within narrowly prescribed limits, tend to be conducted exclusively by those enjoying a degree of official protection, are at best semi-public in nature, and end abruptly when a high-level decision has been reached. Why dissent is more acceptable at these times than at others is something of a mystery, although it may have to do with the competition among those senior officials who aspire to positions of great authority. The airing of different positions may be one way in which the contenders attempt to generate personal support within the political apparatus and to form alliances and coalitions.

The unsettled nature of Kremlin politics in 1982 might have been responsible, at least in part, for the apparent confusion in the Soviet military's assessment of the American military challenge—the tendency both to sound the alarm and to disparage the significance of the problem. Interestingly, the debate became more rather than less intense in 1983, before diminishing somewhat in subsequent years (for reasons to be explored later in the chapter). For the time being, however, the declarations and pronouncements of the Kremlin's most powerful military leaders made for fascinating reading.

Arms Control

In the beginning the Reagan administration's attitude toward U.S.-Soviet arms control was unambiguous: no resumption of negotiations until the modernization and expansion of American military capabilities were well under way—and maybe not even then. It didn't work out that way. The White House soon found itself under considerable pressure both from the American people and from allied governments to return to the bargaining table.

The INF Negotiations

One problem was the projected deployment in Western Europe of some 572 U.S. intermediate-range nuclear forces (so-called INF weapons), scheduled to begin at the end of 1983 unless an agreement to limit these and comparable Soviet weapons could be concluded before that date. The problem had its origins in 1977, when the Kremlin initiated deployment of the SS-20 missile, an extremely accurate, road-mobile weapon system armed with three warheads. Since the United States and its allies had no comparable missile, the SS-20, aimed against targets in Western Europe and the Far East, aroused considerable anxiety in NATO capitals.

As far back as the Carter administration, Western European leaders began to express their concern that unless NATO devised an appropriate response, the Soviet Union would soon enjoy an overwhelming regional nuclear advantage, which it might seek to exploit politically. In Western political and military circles, officials began to discuss the imminent "Finlandization" of the NATO countries in Europe—an allusion to Helsinki's political neutrality and its tendency to refrain from open criticism of Soviet foreign policy.

Initially, the Carter administration resisted European pressures to undertake some kind of countervailing deployments, viewing the installation of additional weapons as militarily unnecessary and the expressions of alarm as unwarranted. The American nuclear guarantee to Europe, administration officials insisted, was as credible as it needed to be. By 1979, however, Washington had changed its mind and the NATO allies agreed to pursue two tracks simultaneously: first, to commit themselves to the deployment of 108 U.S. Pershing II ballistic missiles in the Federal Republic and 464 ground-launched cruise missiles (GLCMs), also under American control, in the United Kingdom, Italy, West Germany, Belgium, and the Netherlands; and second, to propose to the Soviet Union that the two superpowers initiate negotiations as soon as possible to reach an agreement that would eliminate the perceived need to proceed with the missile deployments. For its part, the Kremlin was eager to find some way to prevent or at least reduce the scale of the deployments because of the extended range, great accuracy, and short flight-time of the Pershing II missiles. Preliminary discussions between Washington and Moscow took place in 1980.

The clear preference of many in the Reagan administration, however, was to avoid negotiations altogether and to deploy the missiles. The NATO allies warned the president and his advisers that an American failure to pursue the second part of the "dual track" decision—that is, to negotiate—would be immensely unpopular in Europe and could compel the governments concerned to renege on their commitments to host the new weapons. The administration changed its strategy, albeit reluctantly, and announced in the fall of 1981 that U.S. and Soviet negotiators would meet the following November to explore the possiblity of concluding an agreement to limit intermediate-range nuclear forces.

Two weeks before the start of negotiations, the president previewed the U.S. INF position when he offered to cancel the Pershing II and cruise missile deployments if the Soviet Union would agree to dismantle all 280 SS-20s, as well as some 380 older intermediate-range missile systems. While it was a brilliant diplomatic stroke, the "Zero Option," as the president's plan soon became known, held little appeal for the Kremlin. For one thing, the United States was asking Soviet leaders to dismantle well-over 600 missile systems already located throughout the U.S.S.R. in exchange for which Washington pledged not to deploy the new U.S. weapons in Europe, the first of which were not scheduled to arrive on the continent for another two years.

In addition, Moscow protested that the negotiations were about U.S. and Soviet weapons for use against targets in *Europe* (including the European part of the U.S.S.R.), and not, as the administration claimed, about *all* intermediate-range weapons, including Soviet missiles deployed in Asia. Indicative of the wide gap separating the two sides at the negotiating table was the U.S. claim that the Soviet Union enjoyed a 6 to 1 advantage in INF forces (both missiles and tactical aircraft capable of carrying nuclear weapons), while the Kremlin asserted that the relationship was one of approximate parity. The initial Soviet bargaining posture reflected that calculation, calling for equal numerical reductions over a period of several years. The talks were immediately deadlocked.

The START Talks

Whether to resume negotiations on strategic nuclear forces, in abeyance since the signing of the SALT II treaty in 1979, was a more difficult decision for the administration and came later. Beyond a generalized reluctance to consider new constraints on ICBMs, SLBMs, and long-range bombers, the White House and civilian defense officials were unenthusiastic about SALT-style arms control because of the perception that previous agreements had been advantageous to the Soviet Union. The most the administration was prepared to do concerning SALT II, specifically, was to issue a pledge in mid-1982 that it would not "undercut" the agreement as long as the Soviet Union exercised similar restraint. The Kremlin undertook the same commitment, although U.S. officials charged the Soviets then and later with a host of SALT-related violations. In 1981, the predominant mood within the Reagan White House was to delay the return to the bargaining table for as long as possible, until the United States could deal with the Kremlin "from a position of strength."

By late in the year, however, public opinion data revealed that while the American people were prepared to endorse higher levels of defense spending, they also expected the government to persist in the effort to negotiate some kind of agreement with Moscow to bring the arms race under control. Even more troubling from the administration's perspective, a well-organized and increasingly vocal movement, centered originally in New England but spreading rapidly, was demanding an immediate freeze on the development, testing, production, and deployment of all nuclear weapons and their delivery systems. The brainchild of veteran disarmament activist Randall Forsberg, the freeze movement demonstrated considerable skill in creating a broadly based coalition of anti-nuclear groups, as well as impressive political savvy in its dealings with Congress, especially the House of Representatives. In 1982, Senate and House members introduced the first of several non-binding freeze resolutions. The House version stood a good chance of securing the necessary votes for passage.

Administration spokesmen, starting with the president, counter-attacked, denouncing the freeze as an ill-timed gesture which, if implemented, would condemn the United States to a position of permanent military inferiority. They also lobbied hard to defeat the measure in Congress. The breadth of public support for the freeze, which counted among its adherents prominent members of the Catholic hierarchy, as well as a number of main-line Protestant clergymen and Jewish religious leaders, tended to dilute the moral authority of the president's case.

To relieve the buildup of domestic pressure, reassure nervous allies, and preserve its defense program, the administration sent out strong signals during the spring of 1982 that it would welcome a return to negotiations on strategic nuclear weapons, pending a review of policy and the preparation of an opening proposal. On May 9, in a speech at Eureka College in Illinois, Reagan called on the Kremlin to join the United States in what he termed the Strategic Arms Reduction Talks, or START, at a mutually convenient time and place. The president also outlined the American negotiating position. The United States, Reagan said, looked forward to the conclusion of an agreement that would reduce U.S. and Soviet ICBMs and SLBMs from current levels to no more than 850 for each side (later increased to 1200) and limit ballistic missile warheads to 5000, no more than 2500 of which could be land-based. Significantly, the president proposed no constraints on either long-range bomber forces or cruise missiles, areas in which the United States enjoyed a distinct advantage, later justifying the omission on the grounds that these weapons, which he referred to as "slow flyers," did not pose a first-strike threat.[12]

In the view of senior administration officials, the U.S. START proposals constituted a kind of litmus test of Soviet intentions concerning arms control. They recognized that the reductions outlined by the president would fall more heavily on the Kremlin than on the United States. For example, a ceiling of 850 on long-range ballistic missiles would require the Soviet Union to dismantle almost two-thirds of its ICBMs and SLBMs, while obligating the United States to reduce its forces by half. The proposed sublimit of 2500 on land-based missile warheads would work a similar hardship on the Kremlin, necessitating roughly a 60 percent cut from existing levels; the United States, on the other hand, would be free to increase its holding of ICBM warheads by 350, since in 1982 the total number of Minuteman and

Titan missile reentry vehicles was only 2150. The START proposals were not entirely one-sided, however. Assuming that the United States would divide the allotted number of missile warheads evenly between land- and sea-based forces, Washington would have to scrap approximately half of its 5000 submarine-launched weapons.

The proposals were designed to do several things at once. The first purpose was to underscore the administration's interest in moving beyond what the president and others had described as the mere *regulation* of missile and warhead inventories under SALT to deep *reductions* in weaponry. A second objective was to use the negotiating process to test Moscow's willingness to accept a strict numerical balance in U.S. and Soviet strategic missile forces and warheads. Underlying all was the desire to demonstrate to the American public that the government of Ronald Reagan was making a good faith effort to negotiate with the Soviet Union to bring the arms race under control.

Many in the U.S. arms control community, while praising the president's decision to resume the bargaining process, were sharply critical of the START proposals. Critics focused in particular on the disproportionate nature of the projected reductions and on the initial exclusion of bomber forces. The administration's position, they asserted, was directed more toward influencing American public opinion than to providing a sound basis for negotiating with the Soviet Union. Where were the incentives for Moscow to agree to the plan? Why should the Kremlin consent to reposture its strategic nuclear arsenal, built at enormous expense over twenty years, simply to satisfy U.S. concerns about numerical equality and balance? Why did the proposals not contain constraints on systems that aroused special anxiety in Moscow, such as long-range air-launched cruise missiles? Criticism was also directed at the failure of the proposals to include limitations on the introduction of new weapon systems; under START, each side could continue to deploy generation after generation of advanced ICBMs and SLBMs.

The Kremlin, of course, was even more exercised, denouncing the proposals, in long and detailed analyses on the front pages of *Pravda* and *Izvestiya*, as hopelessly one-sided and prejudicial to Soviet interests. Misgivings aside, the Soviets agreed to dispatch a negotiating team to meet with representatives of the United States. They could do little else in light of the fact that they had repeatedly criticized the Reagan administration for its reluctance to negotiate. On June 29, 1982, in Geneva, the first session of START convened.

From the outset, it was apparent that the positions of the two sides were far apart. The Soviets offered what American officials quickly dubbed a SALT III formula: maintenance of the essential framework of the SALT II treaty, with modest revisions downward in such weapons categories as land-based MIRVed missile systems. The United States presented a more developed version of the president's START proposals. The administration saw the Soviet plan as an unimaginative repackaging of SALT II and an example of incrementalism at its worst. The Kremlin viewed the U.S. proposals as unrealistic and patently non-negotiable. No real bargaining took place, nor could it at this juncture. The two countries weren't even employing the same vocabulary. The Soviets were still pressing for limits on launchers—meaning ICBM silos and the missile tubes on submarines—as in SALT, while the Americans were calling for reductions in missiles and warheads. The first round of START ended in August 1982. Neither side could bring itself to express any genuine optimism as to the pace of the negotiations or the prospects for agreement.

"Ashes, Ashes, All Fall Down"

In 1983, U.S.-Soviet relations hit their lowest point in over two decades. Not that anyone had been expecting a revival of detente. Along virtually every dimension of their relationship, Washington and Moscow seemed to find themselves at odds. The ideological struggle reached new heights with Reagan's "evil empire" speech in March and *Pravda*'s rejoinder that the president suffered from a "pathological disorder." The White House accused the Kremlin of meddling in Central America and the Soviets blamed the insurgency in Afghanistan on the CIA and "imperialist provocateurs" who sent their expense reports to the U.S. Treasury. Bilateral trade, never very extensive, barely topped $2.3 billion in 1983, down from $4.5 billion four years before.

The real fireworks, however, came in three quick bursts: Reagan's "Star Wars" speech in March, the downing of Korean Airlines Flight 007 by Soviet Far Eastern Air Defense Forces in September, and the breaking off of the arms control negotiations in November. Each event, in its own way, said volumes about the superpower relationship.

The Strategic Defense Initiative

At the conclusion of a nationally televised address on March 23 in which he focused on the need for a strong defense, the president first put forth his idea to explore the possibility of creating a comprehensive defensive shield to protect the citizens of the United States from a Soviet missile attack. "Wouldn't it be better," Reagan asked, "to save lives than to avenge them?"[13] From those remarks evolved the Strategic Defense Initiative, more popularly known as SDI or Star Wars. It was a startling proposal—no less so to the president's own staff, many of whom had no advance warning of the announcement, than to the American people at large.

In essence, Reagan was proposing that American scientists begin work on a research program the outcome of which might enable the United States to provide for its security in years to come by relying on strategic defensive capabilities rather than the threat to incinerate the Soviet Union in retaliation for an attack; in other words, to transform the basis of deterrence by replacing *mutual assured destruction* with *mutual assured survival*.

The principal problem with SDI was that no one—least of all the president—knew in 1983 how to defend the American people against Soviet missile forces. When in 1965 then Secretary of Defense McNamara first described the assured destruction capabilities of the two superpowers as the basis of nuclear deterrence, the U.S. strategic arsenal included 850 ICBMs and 500 SLBMs; comparable figures for the Soviet Union were 270 and 120. It was McNamara's considered judgment, shared by most in the American scientific and technical communities, that even with forces of that size neither country could hope to protect more than a fraction of its population through the deployment of anti-ballistic missiles in the event of a large-scale nuclear exchange. McNamara and his deputies also concluded that in a competition between offensive and defensive missile deployments, the former held a distinct advantage because, for the foreseeable future, building more warheads would be cheaper than building more ABM systems.

Less than twenty years later, the number of U.S. and Soviet strategic ballistic missile warheads had increased by a factor of ten, not counting the weapons carried by bombers. Moreover, nothing had been discovered in either American or Soviet weapons laboratories to suggest that what McNamara had deemed impossible in 1965 was suddenly within reach in 1983. Although both Washington and Moscow maintained vigorous research and development programs in strategic defense technologies, the outlook for *effective* nationwide ABM systems, dedicated to the protection of populations, was as bleak as it had ever been.

The president was offering the American people a vision. But it was a vision, to be charitable, without a solid technical foundation. Expressed differently, Reagan had decided, essentially without benefit of counsel, that the basis of U.S. nuclear strategy *should* change without waiting for his technical and military advisers to determine whether it *could* change.

Reaction was immediate and sharply divided. While polling data indicated that the American public would welcome such a shift in U.S. defense policy, there was widespread skepticism that SDI could ever offer reliable protection against an all-out Soviet nuclear attack. For the most part, the scientific and technical communities, including most of the country's most respected physicists with experience in defense-related matters, were either dubious about the feasiblity of the effort or outright hostile. Professional military assessments ranged from enthusiasm in some quarters to expressions of disbelief in others. U.S. allies wondered what the implications of a Fortress America might be for their own security; with the United States at least partially shielded from a nuclear strike, might Washington lose interest in the defense requirements of its friends in Europe and Asia?

Arms control advocates and many defense analysts had a particular set of objections to the Strategic Defense Initiative. They argued with increasing vehemence in the months following the president's announcement that, leaving aside the issues of cost, technical feasibility, and allied anxiety, SDI was a dangerous pipe dream, the most immediate consequence of which would be to render the 1972 ABM treaty a dead letter. It would also make highly unlikely the conclusion of any new U.S.-Soviet agreement to reduce strategic offensive forces. Limiting missile systems was the last thing the Kremlin would be prepared to do in light of the U.S. commitment to explore the possible development of ground- and space-based strategic defenses. The most cost-effective way, they insisted, for Soviet leaders to ensure their military security would be to deploy more and more missiles in order to overwhelm whatever ABM network the Americans eventually decided to build.

In the opinion of most arms controllers, SDI was certain to activate a qualitatively new kind of arms race, one involving the simultaneous procurement of new strategic offensive and defensive forces. Under such conditions, any efforts to regulate the military competition between the superpowers would be an exercise in futility.

The Soviet response bordered on the apoplectic. Four days after the Star Wars speech, a *Pravda* article attributed to General Secretary Andropov condemned the Reagan initiative in the most categorical of terms. "The practical result of this concept," Andropov insisted, ". . . would be to open the floodgates to an unrestrained race in all types of strategic weapons—both offensive and defensive. This is the real meaning . . . of Washington's 'defensive concept.'"

Were it only the prospect of a new arms race, the Kremlin might have been able to contain its wrath. The paramount concern, however, was that the administration had discovered a new vehicle to assist it in the effort to restore American military superiority. The paragraph in which Andropov made this case is worth reproducing in its entirety.

> At first glance, this [the Strategic Defense Initiative] might seem attractive to uninformed people—after all, the President is talking about what seem to be defensive measures. But it seems so only at first glance, and only to those who are unfamiliar with these matters. In fact, the development and improvement of the US's strategic offensive forces will continue at full speed, and in a very specific direction—that of acquiring the potential to deliver a nuclear first strike. In these conditions the intention to obtain the possibility of destroying, with the help of an anti-missile defense, the corresponding strategic systems of the other side, i.e., of depriving it of the capability of inflicting a retaliatory strike, is designed to disarm the Soviet Union in the face of the American nuclear threat.[14]

One did not have to be a Soviet sympathizer to recognize the logic of Andropov's argument. From Moscow's perspective, the Strategic Defense Initiative, in combination with the administration's October 1981 strategic modernization program, could indeed look like a concerted effort to provide the United States with the forces to prevail in the event of nuclear war by depriving the Soviet Union of its ability to retaliate in a convincing manner to an American first strike.

Many in the United States, of course, had identical fears regarding Soviet military intentions. The difference was that the Kremlin had not just announced a major research program along the lines of SDI—although it is important to note in this connection that the Soviets had long maintained an operational ABM capability around Moscow which, in 1983, was in the midst of being upgraded, and were investing billions of rubles in an undeclared SDI-like research program of their own. What seemed to traumatize Kremlin leaders was the fear that the United States might move beyond the developmental phase to the actual deployment of ABM systems before *they* could erect equally effective defensive weapons, leaving the Soviet Union in a militarily inferior position and vulnerable to "nuclear blackmail."

The president went to great lengths to assure the Soviet leadership that his intentions were entirely peaceful, emphasizing that "a nuclear war can never be won and must never be fought." He even offered to make available to the Soviets the necessary technologies to build their own Star Wars defense once the systems had been developed— a gesture Moscow was quick to dismiss as insincere and disingenuous. At the START talks, U.S. negotiators attempted to involve their Soviet colleagues in discussions of how to manage the transition from reliance on strategic offensive forces to a military environment in which defensive weapons would predominate, but the lectures fell on unreceptive ears. A negotiation that had never gotten out of first gear suddenly slipped into reverse.

The Korean Airlines Disaster

The second shock to the superpower relationship in 1983 was a human tragedy that had nothing to do with nuclear weapons or rival conceptions of deterrence. On September 1, a Korean Airlines Boeing 747, carrying 269 passengers (including 61 Americans), en route from the United States to Seoul, departed from its flight path and for two and a half hours overflew militarily sensitive regions of the Soviet Far East. As it was leaving Soviet airspace for the last time, one of three interceptor aircraft that had been converging on the airliner fired a single air-to-air missile which detonated on impact. The crippled 747, which may have disintegrated before impact, plunged into the Sea of Japan. There were no survivors.

A detailed recounting of the Korean Airlines disaster—why the aircraft was off course to begin with, why it failed to take corrective action, why it took Soviet Air Defense Forces over two hours to locate the plane, and why and at what level of decisionmaking Soviet authorities ordered the destruction of the airliner—is beyond the scope of this analysis.[15] What matters in this context was that the episode had a poisonous, if short-term, effect on superpower relations.

The president and Secretary of State George Shultz expressed their outrage, the former characterizing the act as "barbaric," a "massacre," and the work of people who had no respect for innocent human lives. The Soviets, obviously stung, insisted that the airliner had been on a spy mission for American and Korean intelligence services and that the destruction of the plane, while regrettable, was completely justified.

On September 29, Andropov summed up the dismal state of U.S.-Soviet relations in an unusual statement directed to the Soviet people "and all those who are responsible for determining the policies of states." Referring to the alleged role of the United States in masterminding the Korean airlines "spy mission," Andropov pronounced that "If anyone had any illusions concerning the possibility for an evolution for the better in the policies of the current American administration, events of recent times have thoroughly dispelled them. For the sake of achieving its imperial aims, it is going so far that one cannot help but doubt that Washington has any brakes at all to prevent it from crossing the line at which any thinking person should stop."[16] The message was clear but its purpose was vague. Was Andropov announcing a de facto suspension of relations or simply warning the United States that Soviet patience with what he called American adventurism was nearing an end?

The Collapse of the Arms Control Negotiations

It turned out to be a little of both. Two months later, at the end of November, as the first American Pershing II missiles were arriving in Germany, the Soviets walked out of the Geneva negotiations on intermediate-range nuclear forces. The following week they announced that they would not return to the START bargaining table in January when the next round of those negotiations was scheduled to begin. The INF walkout did not come as a total surprise to the United States. Since 1982, Soviet officials had cautioned that they

President Reagan and General Secretary Gorbachev in Geneva, Switzerland, on the afternoon of the first day of Summit talks in November 1985.

would abandon the search for an INF agreement when the first of the new American missiles approached operational readiness. The U.S. position was that the missile deployments would proceed as scheduled but that negotiations should continue.

The talks had gone poorly from the outset, with the United States holding fast to its proposal that the Soviets dismantle all their intermediate-range missiles in exchange for the cancellation of the American missile deployments. A possible compromise, developed by the negotiators during the summer of 1982, was rejected by both governments that fall. Rumors of a breakthrough circulated again the week before the Soviet walkout but they came to nothing in the end.

That the Kremlin also declined to set a date for the resumption of the START talks was more of a jolt to the administration but had little real effect on U.S. conduct. The purpose, after all, was not to force immediate concessions out of Washington but to underscore the depth of Soviet dissatisfaction with the direction of American military policy and the content of its arms control proposals.

On that depressing note, what were arguably the worst twelve months in superpower relations since President Kennedy's first year in office drew to a close.

The Aftermath

Relations between Washington and Moscow improved slightly during 1984, although the turnabout was hardly dramatic. In January Reagan delivered a speech calling for renewed efforts at cooperation in those areas where the United States and the Soviet Union had shared interests. Quiet discussions continued between the two sides on modernizing the Hotline. In February, Andropov died. His successor, Konstantin Chernenko, emphasized the desirability of restoring an element of civility to superpower relations but in light of his demonstrably poor health his power to shape, let alone set, Soviet policy toward the United States was very much in doubt. Finally, in September, during the height of the U.S. presidential campaign, Soviet Foreign Minister Gromyko paid a visit to the White House to consult with Reagan on matters of mutual concern, strongly suggesting that the Kremlin had already decided who was likely to prevail in the November election.

Shortly after Reagan's second inauguration in January 1985, Shultz and Gromyko met in Geneva, agreeing that U.S. and Soviet negotiators would return to the arms control bargaining table in March.

This time, however, there would be three sets of negotiations conducted in parallel: one devoted to the reduction of strategic offensive forces; a second to the limitation of intermediate-range weapons; and a third, at Soviet insistence, to space weapons and defensive systems. Since basically nothing had changed in the fifteen months since the suspension of the original START and INF talks, neither Washington nor Moscow could have anticipated much in the way of quick or substantial progress toward an agreement in any of these complex and interrelated issue areas.

Yet beneath the surface important changes were under way in the relationship, occasioned largely by a modest shift in U.S. policy. Two factors appeared to be at work. The first was the gradual ascendance within the administration of what might be termed greater realism or a less ideological approach to dealing with the Soviets. The president's selection in 1982 of Shultz to succeed Alexander Haig at the State Department began the process, although Shultz moved slowly at first to assert his authority, especially with regard to the politically sensitive questions of superpower relations and arms control policy. By the start of Reagan's second term, however, Shultz had begun to focus on these subjects and his influence was a moderating force. The replacement of William Clark by Robert McFarlane as the president's national security adviser in 1983 brought a second strong centrist voice into the administration's senior policy counsels. One manifestation of the change was the sharp decline after 1983 in the level of Reagan's anti-Sovietism, as expressed in his speeches and press conference performances.

The second factor was economic in character. Congress, finding it difficult to approve large increases in the Defense Department's budget when funding for domestic programs was either stagnant or actually on the decline, served notice during 1985 that future appropriations for the military would henceforth grow at a much more modest pace. This new mood of fiscal austerity, and what it seemed to portend for the pace of the president's defense buildup, tended to make more attractive to at least some members of the administration the conclusion of an arms control agreement with the Soviets. Beginning in 1983, many in Congress worked to strengthen the hand of those within the Executive Branch making this argument.

Just how far the administration had come in its Soviet policy was revealed in November 1985 when Reagan journeyed to Geneva to meet with Mikhail Gorbachev, who had succeeded Chernenko as Communist Party General Secretary in March. The two-day summit accomplished very little, other than to provide an opportunity for the two leaders to get acquainted and to agree to two follow-up meetings, one each in 1986 and 1987. The President and the General Secretary also issued instructions to their arms control negotiators to persist in the search for a new agreement. At least the Reagan-Gorbachev encounter did not precipitate a worsening of relations.

The journey from Reagan's first press conference in January 1981, in which he had insisted that Soviet leaders would lie, cheat, and commit any crime in pursuit of their objectives, to the civil, almost cordial summit meeting in Geneva five years later had been a long one. Despite the softening of the rhetoric and the renewed commitment to negotiate in good faith, however, the two superpowers continued to eye one another with the deepest of suspicion. Although it had started long before, the damage to relations between 1981 and 1985 was so severe that the partial efforts to patch over the rupture constituted little more than cosmetic gestures—welcome, to be sure, but unlikely to promote any lasting or extensive relaxation of tensions.

At root, it was the conviction on each side that the other was unwilling to accept meaningful constraints on the development of its military capabilities, preferring to entrust its security to superiority in weaponry, that made any significant meeting of the minds impossible. Moreover, it was the persistence of the belief within powerful segments of both governments that nuclear weapons were *not* so revolutionary in their implications after all—that a military victory, in other words, could still be obtained through the aggressive application of technology and the allocation of sufficient human and material resources—that ate at the notion of regulating the arms race like a particularly virulent form of cancer. As 1986 began, the prognosis for the patients' eventual recovery was anything but good.

While There Is Still Time / *Bob Salpeter*

7 | Today and Tomorrow

Appearances can be deceiving. Except for a generalized sense that things aren't quite as they should be, most Americans probably don't consider 1986 a particularly noteworthy year in the ongoing effort to control the nuclear arms race. Much the same can be said about the state of U.S.-Soviet relations: While far from warm, relations between Washington and Moscow have at times been much worse. Yet beneath the surface calm critical decisions are being made in both capitals that are likely to have a significant and, in all probability, negative impact on the arms control process and on the future development of relations between the superpowers.

The United States and the Soviet Union are again engaged in formal negotiations to reduce their nuclear weapons stockpiles. These talks, which have been under way since the spring of 1985, are likely to continue for the foreseeable future. That's the good news. There is increasing evidence to suggest, however, that little will come of these deliberations any time soon. As a consequence, the military competition between the two countries will in all probability escalate over the course of the coming decade. That, of course, is the bad news.

The unavoidable conclusion is that the United States and the Soviet Union stand poised on the brink of a qualitatively new round of the arms competition. At a minimum, a no-holds-barred arms race between the superpowers would prove enormously costly. Even more disturbing, such an intensification of the U.S.-Soviet military rivalry—should it develop—would certainly not enhance the security of either; it could, in fact, leave both countries worse off than before.

What are the principal obstacles to the conclusion of a new arms control agreement between Moscow and Washington? What are the possible ramifications of a world *without* such constraints? And what, if anything, might be done over the near- to medium-term to bring the arms race under control and to restore both public and "expert" confidence in the process of negotiating security?

The Current Stalemate

In 1986, the obstacles to significant progress in U.S.-Soviet arms control are many and they operate at several levels. Of these, three are of paramount importance.

The Erosion of Confidence in Negotiated Arms Control

The first obstacle might be termed the "none dare call it treason" syndrome. Two countries locked in a fundamentally adversarial relationship do not often seek to negotiate on security-related issues. In the case of the United States and the Soviet Union, decades of hostility combine with the ability of each to annihilate the other in less than an hour to reinforce this disinclination to bargain. The traditional reflex is to rely on military power—lots of it—to safeguard the security of the state. When negotiations do take place and agreements are concluded, suspicions abound on both sides that such arrangements *must* be flawed or prejudicial to the national interest, almost by definition. Why else would an adversary consent to such accords, if not to attain or preserve a degree of military advantage?

What made possible the conclusion of the 1972 Interim Agreement, the ABM treaty, and SALT II was the temporary suspension of such beliefs on the part of the American and Soviet governments. Put differently, leaders in both countries were prepared to grant that agreements to limit their nuclear weapons arsenals and to constrain various aspects of the military competition *might* be to their mutual advantage—depending of course on the particulars of the agreement or agreements in question.

Central to the success of the SALT process was the conviction that for the time being at least neither superpower was in a position either to establish or to reclaim a position of meaningful nuclear superiority. Informing this judgment was the belief that nuclear weapons had so revolutionized warfare as to deprive the state of the capacity to attain one of its traditional military objectives in the event of conflict, namely the physical defense of the homeland. A society devastated by several thousand nuclear weapons, with perhaps three-quarters of its industry in shambles and a quarter of its population either dead or severely injured, could not be considered to have prevailed in a nuclear war, according to this logic.

By the late 1970s, the validity of this analysis was being seriously questioned in the United States. The core of the criticism was that however Americans and their government might feel about the "nonwinability" of war in the nuclear age, Soviet leaders felt differently. Moreover, it was alleged, the Kremlin was using the arms control negotiations to arrive at militarily advantageous agreements and to lull the United States into a false sense of security, thereby advancing the drive for Soviet military superiority. Many analysts who subscribed to these views moved into positions of authority in the Reagan administration; several of the most prominent remain in office and continue to influence policy.

American critics of arms control hold a range of opinions as to why the negotiating process has failed to serve the national interest. Some argue that because of what they regard as the Kremlin's devotion to the idea that a nuclear war can be fought and won, the United States must be free to deploy whatever forces are required to disabuse the Soviet leadership of these dangerous notions. Previous arms control agreements, the argument continues, have prevented the U.S. government from implementing the full range of military programs essential to deterrence. According to these analysts, arms control has had the perverse effect of *increasing* rather than *decreasing* the likelihood of war. An extreme variant of this position holds that victory in a nuclear war *is* possible, conventional wisdom notwithstanding, and that arms control makes it all but impossible for the United States to acquire the combination of offensive and defensive forces that would permit this country to prevail. For the proponents of either of these two views, the primary consequence of the several SALT agreements has been to lock the United States into a position of military inferiority.

Similar doubts about the potential value of negotiating with the United States have been expressed on occasion by Soviet spokesmen, although seldom so directly. More than a year after Brezhnev signed the first SALT agreements with Nixon in 1972, several senior Soviet analysts took it upon themselves to underscore the danger to Soviet security posed by "warlike circles" in the United States who, despite the negotiations then in progress, had not given up on the pursuit of military superiority. By the early 1980s, such warnings had increased in frequency and become much more focused. Those sounding the alarm also carried greater political weight; Yuri Andropov, for example, struck essentially the same theme in several major speeches and commentaries during his brief tenure as General Secretary of the Soviet Communist Party. The attacks on U.S. defense and arms control policies have yet to subside.

More to the point, until the late 1960s, Soviet military writings routinely endorsed the notion of fighting on to victory in the event of a nuclear war with the West, notwithstanding the "revolutionary implications" of these weapons of mass destruction. Only within the last ten years have these declarations been replaced by frequent high-level statements, military as well as civilian, to the effect that a nuclear exchange between the superpowers would be an unprecedented disaster for both countries. Within this context Soviet leaders from Brezhnev to Gorbachev have attached particular importance to each side's utter vulnerability to retaliation. The problem, of course, for those responsible for the conduct of U.S. defense and arms control policies has been how to assess which of these two very different perspectives corresponds more closely to actual Soviet views.

It is precisely because neither side can be completely confident in its judgment of these matters that both tend to assume the worst and plan accordingly. *It is this dynamic, more than any other, that sustains the nuclear arms race and has made it so difficult to reach even partial agreements to contain the military rivalry between the superpowers.*

In simplified form, this is the situation that exists today. *Each* superpower detects in the military activities of its rival a bid for superiority. *Each* believes the other to be of the opinion that a nuclear war can be fought and won. *Each* sees the arms control proposals of its adversary as insincere and calculated to produce one-sided military advantage. Moreover, there is *enough* evidence that can be mustered in support of these and related propositions to make it impossible for political leaders in either country to dismiss them out of hand.

Once activated, such beliefs tend to acquire a life of their own and to deepen their hold on policymakers over time, even when the data one would assume essential to the rendering of such judgments are

incomplete. Most people are prone to interpret events selectively and to factor out information that contradicts beliefs they hold with particular intensity or conviction. It should come as no surprise that senior government officials are no more immune to such practices than are the rest of us.

Understood in this way, the fact that U.S. and Soviet negotiators have made so little headway in the Geneva negotiations since their resumption in 1985 is perhaps less puzzling. To change the environment at this late date—that is, to break the cycle of distrust—would require decisive political intervention from the highest levels on both sides, as well as a willingness to compromise on a number of critical issues that continue to divide the two countries. Although top level American and Soviet negotiators met during the summer of 1986 specifically to explore whether and under what conditions consensus might be possible, no breakthroughs were reported. As of this writing, there are few external signs that any substantial progress is imminent.

SDI

A second and more tangible obstacle to a new arms control agreement is the problem posed by strategic defenses and, in particular, the administration's strong support of the Strategic Defense Initiative.

However one feels about the technical feasibility of President Reagan's vision, it is apparent that at least in the short run SDI has seriously complicated the negotiations. Among other things, it has reinforced the already strong Soviet suspicion that the overarching objective of U.S. military policy is to attain the capacity to render Soviet nuclear weapons "impotent and obsolete," thereby enabling the United States to prevail over the U.S.S.R., should the two superpowers ever find themselves at war.

Despite the administration's efforts to convince Soviet leaders that the two superpowers can successfully navigate the transition from mutual assured destruction to mutual assured survival, the Kremlin has demonstrated little interest in exploring that option and warns that the inevitable consequence of an American decision to proceed with SDI will be the collapse of the current negotiations to reduce offensive nuclear forces. The Soviets also caution that such a decision will generate irresistible pressures to proliferate the number of nuclear warheads and strategic nuclear delivery vehicles to overcome whatever defensive systems might be deployed, making continued compliance with both the Interim Agreement and SALT II impossible.

The most important casualty of SDI, however, is likely to be the 1972 treaty limiting the deployment of anti-ballistic missile systems. According to administration sources, should the United States proceed with a number of currently-scheduled SDI-related "technology demonstrations," it could be in violation of the ABM treaty as early as 1989. Once this occurs, it is difficult to imagine either side feeling particularly bound by the treaty's provisions or exercising meaningful restraint in the development and testing of ground- and space-based defensive systems. The door would then be open for an unregulated superpower competition in the acquisition of *both* offensive and defensive strategic forces.

An arms race of this kind could prove destabilizing, especially during the so-called transition phase. Were the Soviet Union, for example, to reach the conclusion that within ten to fifteen years the United States could significantly reduce the amount of damage it would sustain in the event of a nuclear exchange, the Kremlin could decide to launch its nuclear forces first in the midst of an extreme superpower crisis if Moscow had reason to believe that the United States was about to "go nuclear." While they could not hope to escape an American counterblow under such circumstances, the Soviets could still decide to undertake such a high-risk strategy in the belief that by striking first *today* they could achieve better military results, relatively speaking, than those likely to obtain *tomorrow*, when they could find themselves at a dramatic military disadvantage.

The scenario may seem farfetched, but it is important to bear in mind that such preventive wars are hardly without precedent. Japan attacked the United States in 1941 at least in part because of Tokyo's calculation that American power, relative to that of Japan, was certain to increase over time. Consequently, the latter was likely to fare better in a war that began sooner rather than later. The fact that Japan lost the war should not obscure the larger point that Japanese leaders made the decision to attack the United States through such reasoning. In what they might regard as a desperate situation, Soviet leaders could decide to do the same.

The more likely scenario, however, is one in which both superpowers proceed to acquire rudimentary anti-ballistic missile defenses as well as additional strategic offensive forces at roughly the same rate, while also developing more exotic means to guarantee that the other side's ABM systems enjoy only limited effectiveness. In this model, neither side would come to possess a decisive military advantage, as both would remain vulnerable to a crippling retaliatory strike. Should this prove to be the case, SDI and its Soviet counterpart would represent less a threat to strategic stability than a colossal waste of resources.

Some U.S. analysts have expressed the view that whatever the operational shortcomings of the president's vision of a nuclear-free world, the Kremlin's fear of SDI seems genuine enough, making it an excellent bargaining chip in the Geneva negotiations. SDI might be extremely useful, in other words, in obtaining the type of arms control agreement that would satisfy even the harshest American critics of the negotiating process.

The argument has merit; the Kremlin has evinced great anxiety about SDI, and since 1983 its arms control proposals have evolved substantially, incorporating a number of elements designed to make the conclusion of a new accord more appealing to the United States. The only weakness in this argument is that the current administration has made it abundantly clear that it has no intention of trading away SDI, even in exchange for deep reductions in Soviet offensive forces. There is little reason to doubt that the president and those who speak on his behalf mean what they say on this score. The Reagan alter-

native is to proceed with SDI research and development while simultaneously beginning the reduction of U.S. and Soviet missiles and bombers—an option the Kremlin has repeatedly denounced as unworkable. The most the administration seems prepared to offer at this stage is continued U.S. compliance with the ABM treaty for a period of up to ten years—after which time each side will be free to deploy such defensive weapons as it sees fit. Since it is unlikely that the United States would be in a position to begin construction of an SDI-like system until *after* the mid-1990s at the earliest, it is difficult to understand why the Kremlin should be any more tempted to accept this offer than those that have hitherto been extended.

What the Soviets have so far failed to achieve, however, Congress might well accomplish. Neither the House nor the Senate has manifested any great enthusiasm for SDI, citing what members of each body have described as a degree of confusion within the administration over the program's exact purposes, feasibility, and cost-effectiveness. As a result, the government's funding requests for SDI have been reduced in each of the last two years. For fiscal year 1987, Congress is likely to appropriate only 60 to 70 percent of the money for which the White House has asked. That pattern will probably persist until such time as the administration can present a more convincing case in support of the program by demonstrating its military utility. Redefining the purpose of SDI—from the defense of cities to the defense of missile silos—is one option for increasing Congressional support for the program since the latter goal presents fewer (although by no means insignificant) technical obstacles and would cost considerably less. To date, however, the White House has manifested little enthusiasm for this so-called "hard-site" mission. Were the administration prepared to use SDI as a bargaining chip, Congress might also allocate additional funds to enhance American negotiating leverage in Geneva, although that is by no means certain.

In the absence of either of these two developments, the administration may well find itself in the awkward position of having committed itself to one of the most dramatic military initiatives in American history—but one that Congress refuses to support at a level commensurate with its alleged significance. In the meantime, the Politburo will be free to allocate whatever funds it deems appropriate for such purposes—in addition to those already earmarked—without having to submit its request to the Supreme Soviet for approval. To compound the problem, should either side decide to abrogate the 1972 ABM treaty, it is the Soviet Union which would be likely to reap the greatest initial benefits, as it is currently in a better position than the United States, according to the Department of Defense, to deploy a nationwide system of anti-ballistic missiles.[1]

For all these reasons, it is difficult to understand why the Reagan administration has been so reluctant to take advantage of whatever leverage SDI provides to cut a deal with Moscow. The president's well-known disinclination to curtail the program is certainly one factor. It also seems that some senior administration officials would prefer that the United States conclude no new agreement with the Kremlin for the remainder of Reagan's term—short of an accord that the Soviet leadership would almost certainly regard as detrimental to its security.

The Compliance Issue

The third obstacle is what administration spokesmen characterize as a "pattern" of Soviet non-compliance with existing arms control agreements. Since 1984, the White House has issued a series of reports alleging that the Soviet Union has violated key provisions of several important accords, including the Interim Agreement, the ABM treaty, and SALT II. The Kremlin, claiming that it faithfully abides by the terms of these agreements, denies all charges, and points an accusing finger at the United States for what it describes as a dismal record on compliance. To level such charges is a serious matter and both sides have been criticized for the highly public manner in which they have sought to make their case and for their willingness to politicize such a sensitive issue.

The administration attaches particular importance to three alleged violations. The first concerns the large, phased-array radar that the Soviets are constructing in central Siberia in apparent contravention of the ABM treaty. While that agreement does not prohibit the building of such facilities, it does require that they be located on the periphery of U.S. and Soviet territory and "oriented outward." The constraints are designed to ensure that these very capable radars will be used only for early warning of ballistic missile attack, and not for the purpose of directing anti-ballistic missiles to their targets—the so-called ABM "battle management" function. The radar in question, which the Soviets insist is for the tracking of space vehicles, is, in the opinion of some U.S. analysts, well positioned for the second and prohibited of these missions. While the radar's military significance is at this point marginal, the administration contends that its construction reveals the Kremlin's willingness to disregard treaty commitments when it is militarily advantageous to do so.

The second case centers on a new Soviet single-warhead missile, known in the West as the SS-25. The SALT II treaty limits each side to one new type of long-range land based missile. The Soviets have identified the MIRVed SS-24 (the first of which are likely to be deployed at the end of 1986) as their "new" missile and the SS-25 (approximately 70 of which are already operational) as a permissible modification of an existing type. The United States rejects the Soviet claim, alleging that various parameters of the SS-25 differ significantly from the missile to which it is being compared. Neither country appears ready to concede on this issue.

The third "violation" has to do with the coding or encryption of data from missile flight tests. SALT II obligated the signatories to refrain from the "deliberate denial of telemetric information" during the testing of ICBMs and SLBMs, whenever such action would impede verification of compliance with the provisions of the treaty.

During missile tests, great amounts of information are relayed to ground stations monitoring the launch. Much of that data is picked up by the other side through electronic eavesdropping. The country conducting the launch can encrypt much of this information, making it all but impossible for the other side to decipher it. Without access to these communications, the country observing the launch cannot determine many of the characteristics of the missile system in question and therefore cannot reliably gauge whether the side conducting the test is in compliance with the relevant terms of the agreement.

The administration alleges that Soviet encryption practices make effective monitoring impossible. The Soviets reject the charge and deny that they are engaging in the deliberate denial of important information. They have also invited the administration to state its precise needs in this area—an offer the U.S. government has declined to accept for fear of revealing shortcomings in its intelligence gathering capabilities.

The resolution of all these controversies involves highly technical judgments, and, in several of the cases, requires access to classified information. Even those in a position to assess the evidence have reached varying conclusions as to the merits of each of these charges.

The administration has publicized the dispute over compliance with two ends in mind: to generate pressure on the Soviet Union to cease certain activities to which the U.S. government takes exception, and to build the case against continued American compliance. Why should the United States comply with the provisions of the signed but unratified SALT II treaty, for example, when the Soviets have violated a number of its provisions?

Those who oppose administration policy on this issue respond in two ways. First, as Robert McNamara has observed, to reason in this way is comparable to throwing out the criminal code because someone commits a crime. The more appropriate response is to assess the military significance of each purported violation on a case by case basis and to weigh carefully the *costs* of continued compliance against the *benefits*. If it can be determined that staying within the limits of a given agreement serves the national interest by placing equal or greater restrictions on the adversary, then continuing to honor that accord makes sense—as long as the violations attributed to the other side are determined to be minor or militarily insignificant in nature. The second response focuses on the use of what is typically called private rather than public diplomacy to resolve disputes of this kind. For those who argue in this way, the proper mechanism for addressing these compliance issues is the U.S.-Soviet Standing Consultative Commission, which was created in the wake of SALT I specifically for this purpose. The administration takes particular exception to this proposal, arguing that despite repeated attempts to resolve these questions through the SCC, the problems persist.

In May 1986 the White House released a statement to the effect that in light of Soviet non-compliance, the United States would not base future decisions concerning strategic weapons deployments on the issue of whether or not such actions might constitute a violation of SALT II. At the same time, the administration seemed to leave itself room to maneuver on the matter by noting that it was prepared to reconsider its decision should the Soviet Union utilize the six months before the end of 1986 to demonstrate a renewed commitment to abide by the agreement's terms. As of this writing, the future of SALT II remains very much in doubt, with the United States scheduled to exceed by late in the year the agreement's aggregate ceiling on multiple-warhead ICBM and SLBM launchers and B-52 aircraft equipped with air-launched cruise missiles.

The controversy over compliance—and the relationship between compliance with existing arms control agreements and the conclusion of new ones—shows no signs of abating. If anything, the dispute is becoming more intense. The most unfortunate aspect of this debate is that it has little bearing on the potential utility of any future agreements. The issue is not so much whether the Soviet Union has cheated on previous accords—however regrettable we find such activity—as it is how to prevent the recurrence of such incidences. A second and related issue is how to design better agreements: how to draw up treaties, in other words, that limit both sides' temptation to engage in practices that might arouse suspicion and distrust. The most important requirement in this regard is that the United States not become party to any arms control accord that cannot be monitored with high reliability through so-called national technical means, supplemented by such cooperative measures as the two countries are willing to accept, including some forms of on-site inspection. Judging some aspects of previous agreements to be lacking in verifiability is no justification for abandoning the arms control process altogether.

Getting Back on Track

The combination of these three powerful obstacles—the general-ized sense of distrust that has emerged on both sides, the prob-lems associated with strategic defenses, and the dispute over com-pliance—strongly suggest that no new, comprehensive agreement to reduce strategic nuclear weapons is likely to be concluded in the near future. Other, so-called interim measures to limit one or an-other *aspect* of the superpower military rivalry cannot be ruled out, although even on this front success is far from assured.

In the near term, the goal should be to keep things from getting any worse. Among the steps that should be taken to prevent any additional erosion of the arms control agreements already in place:

- *Both sides should reaffirm their commitment to abide by the terms of the ABM treaty and renew their pledge not to undercut the provisions of either the 1972 Interim Agreement or SALT II.* These agreements, while far from perfect, contain impor-tant constraints on the development and deployment of strategic defensive and offensive weapons systems. They also provide a framework or a baseline for the conclusion of future agreements. They do not prevent the United States from taking prudent steps to safeguard its security and that of its allies; in addition, they enable U.S. military planners to estimate the nature and scope of the Soviet military chal-lenge more effectively than would otherwise be the case.

- *Any SDI-related technology demonstrations that would violate the ABM treaty should be deferred, pending the renegotiation of the treaty, or postponed indefinitely.* Once the treaty has been violated, it could prove impossible to salvage. The result would likely be an accelerated Soviet ABM program, the collapse of the constraints on strategic offensive forces, and a qualitative and quantitative arms race that neither side could hope to win. Moreover, there is no pressing *military* need to test SDI components or subsystems between now and the end of the decade.

• *Redouble the effort to resolve the dispute over compliance.* American public faith in arms control will not be restored until charges of Soviet noncompliance have been properly dealt with and, to the extent possible, resolved to the satisfaction of both parties. The administration should desist in its highly public attacks on Soviet practices in this regard—which only stiffen Moscow's resistance to comply with the U.S. demands—and continue to seek resolution through diplomatic channels.

Over the longer term, it is vitally important that the United States and the Soviet Union persist in the effort to negotiate an absolute ceiling on the number of strategic nuclear delivery vehicles and warheads and then move on to deep reductions. Both sides have committed themselves to reductions on the order of 50 percent, which is an appropriate and achievable mid-range objective. Such a goal can only be realized, however, if Washington and Moscow agree to defer the development of sophisticated strategic defensive technologies until far into the future, when the number of offensive weapons has been reduced from tens of thousands to several hundred. It is only in such an environment that SDI-like defenses might afford both countries a meaningful degree of protection against missile-borne nuclear weapons. The two superpowers should also explore ways to reduce the most menacing components of their strategic nuclear arsenals: the extremely high-accuracy, multiple-warhead missiles that threaten each other's retaliatory forces. An agreement to de-MIRV ICBMs and SLBMs, for instance, would greatly strengthen deterrence.

Two final points deserve to be made in considering the future of arms control and of U.S.-Soviet relations. The first is the elementary but frequently overlooked observation that as Washington and Moscow attempt to negotiate on security related issues, they do so as adversaries, not as friends. While leaders in both countries should work for a diminution of the political differences that separate the two superpowers, the United States and the Soviet Union are not about to sign a treaty of friendship and mutual assistance. As a consequence, such progress as they achieve in arms control is always incremental and only occasionally significant. Their mutual hostility has been two generations in the making and it is unreasonable to expect them to score spectacular gains overnight.

What implications flow from this observation? For one thing, Americans must learn to be patient with the process and to assess whatever agreements are forthcoming not against some absolute standard—such as whether this will achieve disarmament—but against present-day realities. The question is not "Will this agreement abolish nuclear weapons?" but "Will this agreement reduce the likelihood of nuclear war, facilitate the conclusion of additional accords, and enhance U.S. national security?" If the answer to the second question is "Yes," then the agreement deserves support.

We must also resist the temptation to look for technological solutions to what are essentially political problems. As this study has sought to demonstrate, nuclear weapons *are* different from the weapons that have come before, they *have* transformed the nature of war, and they *have* revolutionized the conduct of military operations and international relations. Their effects cannot be minimized simply by thinking of them as more powerful versions of conventional armaments. The answer to the nuclear predicament does not lie in technological wizardry.

In defense of SDI, some proponents have been moved to cite the example of the Apollo space program, which put Americans on the moon. As the distinguished physicist Sidney Drell has remarked, the analogy is less than apt; after all, the moon didn't shoot back. This is not to suggest that the government should abandon the search for technologies which might improve U.S. national security. It is to suggest, however, that we should keep our enthusiasm for such ventures in perspective, recognizing the value of other, less compelling but equally important, techniques for accomplishing the same objective, such as direct negotiations with the Soviet Union.

The second major point to keep in mind is that arms control has its own set of problems as a mechanism to limit the nuclear competition. In at least one sense, President Reagan's characterization of the SALT II treaty as flawed is correct, although not in the sense he meant. The agreement is flawed because the process which spawned it has a number of shortcomings. Foremost among these has been the tendency of the two superpowers both to acquire and to retain weapons systems for the purpose of increasing their bargaining leverage. The MX missile is frequently justified on these grounds: that the United States needs the weapon in order to demonstrate national resolve and to provide an incentive for the Soviets to negotiate in earnest. The fact that the MX in reconditioned Minuteman silos cannot perform one of the two missions for which it was built—to survive a Soviet ICBM attack—has become a secondary consideration. Formalized negotiations can contribute, in other words, to a vicious cycle in which each participant deploys weapons that it may not want but believes it must have in order to obtain a desirable outcome. Observing such activity, the other side feels compelled to do the same.[2] The SALT process has also made both countries more sensitive than they might otherwise have been to the exact composition of the strategic military balance, especially to what are known as static indicators, such as the number of missiles, bombers, and warheads on each side.

The problem is serious but perhaps not insurmountable. One solution might be to impose a temporary freeze on the procurement and deployment of strategic weapons systems at the outset of formal negotiations. The major complication is timing: One side will very likely allege that it is behind the other in some important index of military power and resist such a move. Strong political leadership can sometimes overcome domestic opposition of this kind, although frequently not without a struggle.

A second and more difficult option is to combine negotiations with what is described in the literature of the defense and arms control communities as unilateral restraint. Examples might include a decision not to deploy the MX because of its vulnerability, or to forego the Trident II SLBM because of the threat it would pose to Soviet land-based missiles. A more radical proposal would be to reduce the total number of U.S. strategic weapon systems and warheads by 25 to 50 percent, without waiting for an agreement with Moscow, making sure that the remaining American forces could not be destroyed in a Soviet first strike.

Beyond the political opposition that would be certain to develop in the event of such a profound restructuring of the U.S. deterrent, this approach has the particular drawback of virtually eliminating any Soviet incentive to negotiate. However, if one believes—as this author does—that the nuclear balance is relatively insensitive to numbers and that 5000 modern nuclear warheads, deployed in a variety of highly survivable basing modes, constitute an adequate deterrent, then this approach has considerable appeal, whatever the Soviet leadership might decide to do.

It is worth bearing in mind, however, that scholars, unlike politicians, do not govern; they are free, therefore, to offer their individual recommendations on how to bring the nuclear arms race under control without excessive regard for public opinion.

In the "real world," national leaders are almost always constrained by political pressures that limit their freedom to maneuver and to undertake bold initiatives. This is especially true in a democratic society such as our own. On balance, Americans prefer it that way except, of course, when presidential or Congressional timidity affects an issue about which we hold firm views. A more explicit recognition of this fact—that national policy almost always changes slowly and only after the sustained application of political pressure—could vastly improve the ability of various citizens' groups, including those favoring substantial progress in arms control, to realize their goals.

In the end, each American must make up his or her own mind about how best to provide for the national security, while at the same time reducing the likelihood of war. For some, the answer is to be found in the restoration of American military superiority. For others, the only hope lies in disarmament. This book has attempted to explain why neither goal is likely to be attained in the near future and to suggest yet a third course.

Issues relating to war and peace matter to each of us at such a profound level that our judgments are often more intuitive than reasoned. The purpose of this book has been to supplement instinct with fact, to inform rather than persuade, and to raise at least as many questions as it answers. If we are to survive the nuclear revolution, we must first educate ourselves to its essential nature. The second step is to make certain that those we elect to high office have received a similar education. The third step is to communicate our views—directly, intelligently, persuasively, and incessantly—to those we have chosen to represent us. More than our right, it is our democratic duty.

Notes

Getting Started

1 Harold Willens, *The Trimtab Factor: How Business Executives Can Help Solve the Nuclear Crisis* (New York: William Morrow, 1984), inside front cover.
2 Freeman Dyson, *Weapons and Hope* (New York and Cambridge: Harper and Row, 1984).

Chapter 1

1 Hans Morgenthau, *Politics Among Nations: The Struggle for Power and Peace*, 3rd ed. (New York: Knopf, 1960), first published in 1948, remains one of the definitive works of the Realist school. For an excellent overview, see Chapter 1, "Six Principles of Political Realism," pp. 14–16.
2 Robert Jervis has written extensively on many aspects of modern international relations and on the "security dilemma" in particular. See especially "Cooperation Under the Security Dilemma," *World Politics*, vol. 30 (January 1978); and, more recently, "From Balance to Concert: A Study of International Security Cooperation," *World Politics*, vol. 38 (October 1985).
3 Robert Axelrod, *The Evolution of Cooperation* (New York: Basic Books, 1984), pp. 27–38.
4 John Lewis Gaddis, *Strategies of Containment: A Critical Appraisal of Postwar National Security Policy* (New York and Oxford: Oxford University Press, 1982).
5 The causes of the Cuban missile crisis and the factors that led to its resolution continue to be the subject of heated scholarly debate. One of the most exhaustive analyses is Graham T. Allison, *Essence of Decision: Explaining the Cuban Missile Crisis* (Boston and Toronto: Little, Brown, 1971). For an examination of Soviet perspectives on the installation of the missiles in Cuba and the ensuing crisis, see Adam Ulam, *Expansion and Coexistence: Soviet Foreign Policy 1917–1973*, 2nd ed. (New York: Holt, Rinehart and Winston, 1974), pp. 667–77.
6 For an outstanding and comprehensive treatment of this subject, see Robert Jervis, *Perception and Misperception in International Politics*. (Princeton, NJ: Princeton University Press, 1976). See also Richard Ned Lebow, *Between Peace and War: The Nature of International Crisis* (Baltimore and London: Johns Hopkins University Press, 1981).

Chapter 2

1 As quoted in Coral Bell, *The Conventions of Crisis: A Study in Diplomatic Management* (New York and Oxford: Oxford University Press, 1971), p. 2.
2 Of the several current studies on the potential environmental consequences of nuclear war, the first three sections of Carl Sagan, "Nuclear War and Climatic Catastrophe: Some Policy Implications," *Foreign Affairs*, vol. 62 (Winter 1983-84), provide an excellent general discussion. For more detailed studies, see R.P. Turco, O.B. Toon, T.P. Ackerman, J.B. Pollack, and Carl Sagan, "Nuclear Winter: Global Consequences of Multiple Nuclear Explosions," *Science*, vol. 222 (December 23, 1983); and Samuel Glasstone and P.J. Dolan, eds., *The Effects of Nuclear Weapons* (Washington, D.C.: U.S. Government Printing Office, 1977).
3 The letter, signed by Oppenheimer, Oliver Buckley, Hartley Rowe, Cyril Smith, L.A. DuBridge, and James Conant, appears as an addendum to the "Report to the General Advisory Committee to the United States Atomic Energy Commission (Historical Document #349, October 30, 1949)." See Herbert York, *The Advisors: Oppenheimer, Teller and the Superbomb* (San Francisco: W.H. Freeman, 1976), pp. 156–57.

4   Sidney D. Drell, Philip J. Farley, and David Holloway, *The Reagan Strategic Defense Initiative: A Technical, Political, and Arms Control Assessment* (Stanford, CA: Center for International Security and Arms Control, 1984) provides one of the most comprehensive analyses currently available of the potential military and political implications of SDI.

5   For a discussion of U.S. decisionmaking during the 1961 Berlin crisis, see Robert M. Slusser, "The Berlin Crises of 1958-59 and 1961," in Barry M. Blechman and Stephen S. Kaplan, et al., *Force Without War: U.S. Armed Forces as a Political Instrument* (Washington, D.C.: Brookings Institution, 1978), especially pp. 397–430.

6   An excellent and detailed account of U.S.–Soviet interaction during the October 1973 war in the Middle East can be found in Raymond L. Garthoff, *Detente and Confrontation: American-Soviet Relations from Nixon to Reagan* (Washington, D.C.: Brookings Institution, 1985), pp. 360–405.

7   See Alexander L. George, "The Basic Principles Agreement of 1972: Origins and Expectations," in Alexander L. George, et al., *Managing U.S.–Soviet Rivalry: Problems of Crisis Prevention* (Boulder, CO: Westview Press, 1983), pp. 107–118.

Chapter 3

1   See John Lewis Gaddis, *The United States and the Origins of the Cold War, 1941–47* (New York: Columbia University Press, 1972), especially Chapter 4, "Repression Versus Rehabilitation: The Problem of Germany."

2   For a closer look at the Potsdam conference, see Herbert Feis, *Between War and Peace: The Potsdam Conference* (Princeton, NJ: Princeton University Press, 1960); and Gabriel Kolko, *The Politics of War: The World and United States Foreign Policy, 1943–1945* (New York: Vintage Books, 1968), pp. 568–93.

3   Perhaps the best analysis of Kennan's conception of U.S. foreign policy and the challenges posed by the Soviet Union is found in Gaddis, *Strategies of Containment* (see Note 4, Chapter 1). See also John Lewis Gaddis, "Containment: A Reassessment," *Foreign Affairs*, vol. 55 (July 1977).

4   Robert D. Schulzinger, *American Diplomacy in the Twentieth Century* (New York and Oxford: Oxford University Press, 1984), p. 222. For a firsthand account of Senator Taft's opposition to U.S. involvement in NATO, see Robert A. Taft, *A Foreign Policy For Americans* (Garden City, NY: Doubleday, 1951), pp. 89–96.

5   See Dean Acheson, *Present at the Creation: My Years in the State Department* (New York: W.W. Norton, 1969), p. 377; and Paul Y. Hammond, "NSC–68: Prologue to Rearmament," in Warner Schilling, Paul Y. Hammond, and Glenn H. Snyder, *Strategy, Politics, and Defense Budgets* (New York: Columbia University Press, 1962), pp. 318–19, 344.

6   The text of NSC-68 can be found in Thomas H. Etzold and John Lewis Gaddis, eds., *Containment: Documents on American Policy and Strategy 1945–1950* (New York: Columbia University Press, 1978), pp. 385–442. The quotation cited appears on p. 412.

7   For a detailed account of the Eisenhower administration's military strategy, especially regarding nuclear weapons, see George H. Quester, *Nuclear Diplomacy: The First Twenty-Five Years* (New York: Dunellen, 1970), pp. 89–144.

8   Robert J. Art and Kenneth N. Waltz, eds., *The Use of Force: International Politics and Foreign Policy* (Boston: Little, Brown, 1971), p. 131.

9   See Herbert S. Dinerstein, *War and the Soviet Union: Nuclear Weapons and the Revolution in Soviet Military and Political Thinking* (New York: Praeger, 1962), especially pp. 71–77.

Chapter 4

1   Ulam, *Expansion and Coexistence*, pp. 588–89. (See Chapter 1, note 5.)

2   For a discussion of the transition from "general and complete disarmament" to arms control, see Coit D. Blacker and Gloria Duffy, eds., *International Arms Control: Issues and Agreements*, 2nd ed. (Stanford, CA: Stanford University Press, 1984), pp. 107–112.

3   An excellent analysis of U.S. defense-decisionmaking in the early 1960s can be found in Alain C. Enthoven and K. Wayne Smith, *How Much Is Enough? Shaping the Defense Program,*

1961-1969 (New York: Harper and Row, 1971). Regarding the composition of the U.S. strategic arsenal, see especially pp. 165–96.

4   *The Military Balance, 1972–1973* (London: Institute for Strategic Studies, 1972), p. 67.
5   David Holloway, *The Soviet Union and the Arms Race* (New Haven, CT: Yale University Press, 1983), pp. 39–40.
6   *Ibid.*, p. 40.
7   For two excellent treatments of the evolution of U.S. military doctrine and the advent of "flexible response," see Lawrence Freedman, *The Evolution of Nuclear Strategy* (New York: St. Martins Press, 1983), pp. 372–95; and Michael Nacht, *The Age of Vulnerability: Threats to the Nuclear Stalemate* (Washington, D.C.: Brookings Institution, 1985), pp. 87–95.
8   John Newhouse, *Cold Dawn: The Story of SALT* (New York: Holt, Rinehart and Winston, 1973), pp. 94–96.

Chapter 5

1   Garthoff, *Detente and Confrontation*. (See Chapter 2, note 6.)
2   Zbigniew Brzezinski, *Power and Principle: Memoirs of the National Security Advisor 1977–1981* (New York: Farrar, Straus & Giroux, 1983), p. 189.
3   Garthoff, *Detente and Confrontation*, pp. 127–32.
4   See Blacker and Duffy, *International Arms Control*, pp. 225–27. (See Chapter 4, note 2.)
5   Philip Farley discusses Semenov's characterization of the nature of the offense–defense relationship in his chapter, "Strategic Arms Control," in a forthcoming book on U.S.–Soviet security cooperation, edited by Alexander Dallin, Farley, and Alexander L. George.
6   The text of the ABM Treaty can be found in *Arms Control and Disarmament Agreements: Texts and Histories of Negotiations* (Washington, D.C.: U.S. Government Printing Office, 1982), pp. 139–47.
7   For a thorough treatment of the Interim Agreement (Between the United States of America and the Union of Soviet Socialist Republics on Certain Measures with Respect to the Limitation of Strategic Offensive Arms), see Blacker and Duffy, *International Arms Control*, pp. 229–34.
8   *Ibid.*, pp. 247–49.
9   See Coit D. Blacker, "The Kremlin and Detente: Soviet Conceptions, Hopes, and Expectations," in George, *Managing U.S.–Soviet Rivalry*, pp. 119–38. (See Note 7, Chapter 2.)
10 For a discussion of the difficulties associated with the practical application of a crisis–management regime, see Alexander L. George, "The Arab–Israeli War of October 1973: Origins and Impact," in George, *Managing U.S.–Soviet Rivalry*, pp. 139–54.
11 See Blacker, "The Kremlin and Detente," in George, *Managing U.S.–Soviet Rivalry*, especially pp. 126–29.
12 See, for example, Paul H. Nitze, "Assuring Strategic Stability in an Era of Detente," *Foreign Affairs*, vol. 54 (January 1976), especially pp. 225–28.
13 The text of the SALT II treaty can be found in *Arms Control and Disarmament Agreements: Text and Histories of Negotiations*, pp. 246–69.
14 Gloria Duffy has done extensive work on the "rediscovery" of the Soviet combat brigade in Cuba in 1979 and the impact that incident had on prospects for the ratification of the SALT II treaty. See, in particular, "Crisis Mangling and the Cuban Brigade," *International Security*, vol. 62 (Summer 1983).
15 Robert Jervis, "Security Regimes," in Stephen D. Krasner, ed., *International Regimes* (Ithaca and London: Cornell University Press, 1983), p. 173.

Chapter 6

1   "The President: News Conference of January 29 (Excerpts)," *Department of State Bulletin*, vol. 81 (March 1981), p. 12.
2   *Ibid.*
3   Georgi Arbatov, "The U.S.—Will There Be Changes?" *Pravda*, March 17, 1983.

4 Ronald Reagan, "Promoting Democracy and Peace," British Parliament, London, June 8, 1982, *Realism, Strength, Negotiation: Key Foreign Policy Statements of the Reagan Administration* (Washington, D.C.: U.S. Department of State, Bureau of Public Affairs, 1984), pp. 77–81.

5 "Excerpts From President's Speech to National Association of Evangelicals," *New York Times*, March 9, 1983.

6 Jimmy Carter, "A Foreign Policy Based on America's Fundamental Character," May 22, 1977, *Department of State Bulletin*, vol. 76 (June 13, 1977), p. 622.

7 *Report of the Secretary of Defense Caspar W. Weinberger to the Congress on the FY 1984 Budget, FY 1985 Authorization Request and FY 1984–88 Defense Programs*, February 1, 1983 (Washington, D.C.: U.S. Government Printing Office, 1983), p. 51.

8 *Ibid.*, p. 55.

9 *Ibid.*, p. 32.

10 Dmitry Ustinov, "To Avert the Threat of Nuclear War," *Pravda*, July 12, 1982.

11 "Marshall of the Soviet Union D.F. Ustinov, USSR Minister of Defense, Answers Questions from a Pravda Correspondent," *Pravda*, December 7, 1982.

12 Ronald Reagan, "Arms Control and the Future of East-West Relations," Eureka College Commencement, Peoria, Illinois, May 9, 1982, *Realism, Strength, Negotiation: Key Foreign Policy Statements of the Reagan Administration*, pp. 27–30.

13 Ronald Reagan, "Peace and National Security," televised address to the nation, Washington, D.C., March 23, 1983, *Realism, Strength, Negotiation: Key Foreign Policy Statements of the Reagan Administration*, pp. 37–43.

14 "Yu.V. Andropov Answers Questions from a Pravda Correspondent," *Pravda*, March 27, 1983.

15 For an excellent and very readable account of the Korean Airlines disaster, see Alexander Dallin, *Black Box: KAL 007 and the Superpowers* (Los Angeles and Berkeley: University of California Press, 1985).

16 "Statement By Yu.V. Andropov, General Secretary of the CPSU Central Committee and Chairman of the Presidium of the USSR Supreme Soviet," *Pravda*, September 29, 1983.

Chapter 7

1 See Caspar Weinberger, *Report of the Secretary of Defense Caspar W. Weinberger to the Congress on the FY 1987 Budget, FY 1988 Authorization Request and the FY 1987–91 Defense Programs*, February 5, 1986 (Washington, D.C.: U.S. Government Printing Office, 1986), p. 77. For a more extensive look at the Reagan administration's assessment of Soviet ABM capabilities, see *Soviet Military Power 1986*, 5th ed. (Washington, D.C.: U.S. Government Printing Office, 1985), pp. 41–57.

2 See Jane M.O. Sharp, "Restructuring the SALT Dialogue," *International Security*, vol. 6 (Winter 1981–82), pp. 144–76. There is a good deal of methodologically sophisticated literature on negotiating behavior; a particularly accessible introduction to the topic is James A. Wall, *Negotiating Theory and Practice* (Glenview, IL: Scott, Foresman, 1985). On this subject, I am grateful to Phil Ellis for sharing with me his work on "bargaining chips."

Suggested Reading

U.S. Foreign and Military Policy

Blechman, Barry M. and Stephen S. Kaplan, et al. *Force Without War: U.S. Armed Forces as a Political Instrument*. Washington, D.C.: The Brookings Institution, 1978.

Brown, Harold. *Thinking About National Security: Defense and Foreign Policy in a Dangerous World*. Boulder, CO: Westview Press, 1983.

Etzold, Thomas H. and John Lewis Gaddis, eds. *Containment: Documents on American Policy and Strategy, 1945–1950*. New York: Columbia University Press, 1978.

Gaddis, John Lewis. *Strategies of Containment: A Critical Appraisal of Postwar National Security Policy*. New York and Oxford: Oxford University Press, 1982.

George, Alexander L., and Richard Smoke. *Deterrence in American Foreign Policy: Theory and Practice*. New York: Columbia University Press, 1974.

Kennan, George F. *Memoirs 1925–1950*. Boston and Toronto: Little, Brown, 1967.

Kissinger, Henry. *The White House Years*. Boston and Toronto: Little, Brown, 1979.

Kissinger, Henry. *Years of Upheaval*. Boston and Toronto: Little, Brown, 1982.

Schulzinger, Robert D. *American Diplomacy in the Twentieth Century*. New York and Oxford: Oxford University Press, 1984.

Soviet Foreign and Military Policy

Bialer, Seweryn. *The Soviet Paradox: External Expansion, Internal Decline*. New York: Alfred A. Knopf, 1986.

Holloway, David. *The Soviet Union and the Arms Race*. New Haven, CT: Yale University Press, 1983.

Kaplan, Stephen S., et al. *Diplomacy of Power: Soviet Armed Forces as a Political Instrument*. Washington, D.C.: The Brookings Institution, 1981.

Ulam, Adam. *Expansion and Coexistence: Soviet Foreign Policy 1917–1973*. 2d ed. New York: Holt Rinehart and Winston, 1974.

Ulam, Adam. *Dangerous Relations: The Soviet Union and World Politics, 1970–1982*. New York and Oxford: Oxford University Press, 1983.

American-Soviet Relations

Garthoff, Raymond. *Detente and Confrontation: American Soviet Relations from Nixon to Reagan*. Washington, D.C.: The Brookings Institution, 1985.

George, Alexander L., *Managing U.S.-Soviet Rivalry: Problems of Crisis Prevention*. Boulder, CO: Westview Press, 1983.

Arms Control and Nuclear Weapons

Allison, Graham T., Albert Carnesale and Joseph S. Nye, Jr., eds. *Hawks, Doves and Owls: An Agenda for Avoiding Nuclear War*. New York: W.W. Norton, 1985.

Blacker, Coit D., and Gloria Duffy, eds., *International Arms Control: Issues and Agreements*, 2nd ed. Stanford, CA: Stanford University Press, 1984.

Drell, Sidney. *Facing the Threat of Nuclear Weapons*. Seattle and London: University of Washington Press, 1983.

Jervis, Robert. *The Illogic of American Nuclear Strategy*. Ithaca and London: Cornell University Press, 1984.

Kaplan, Fred M. *The Wizards of Armageddon*. New York: Simon and Schuster, 1983.

Mandelbaum, Michael. *The Nuclear Future*. Ithaca and London: Cornell University Press, 1983.

Mandelbaum, Michael. *The Nuclear Question: The United States and Nuclear Weapons, 1946–1976*. Cambridge and New York: Cambridge University Press, 1979.

Nacht, Michael. *The Age of Vulnerability: Threats to the Nuclear Stalemate*. Washington, D.C.: The Brookings Institution, 1985.

Newhouse, John. *Cold Dawn: The Story of SALT*. New York: Holt, Rinehart and Winston, 1973.

Quester, George H. *Nuclear Diplomacy: The First Twenty-Five Years*. New York: Dunellen Publishing Company, 1970.

Smith, Gerard. *Doubletalk: The Story of the First Strategic Arms Limitation Talks*. Garden City, NY: Doubleday, 1980.

Talbott, Strobe. *Endgame: The Inside Story of SALT II*. New York: Harper Colophon Books, 1979.

Talbott, Strobe. *Deadly Gambits: The Reagan Administration and The Stalemate in Nuclear Arms Control*. New York: Knopf, 1984.

York, Herbert. *Race to Oblivion: A Participant's View of the Arms Race*. New York: Simon and Schuster, 1970.

International Relations Theory

Axelrod, Robert. *The Evolution of Cooperation*. New York: Basic Books, 1984.

Jervis, Robert. *Perception and Misperception in International Politics*. Princeton, NJ: Princeton University Press, 1976.

Morgenthau, Hans. *Politics Among Nations: the Struggle for Power and Peace*, 3rd ed. New York: Knopf, 1960.

Glossary of Terms

ABM	Antiballistic missile
ACDA	Arms Control and Disarmament Agency
ALCM	Air-launched cruise missile
ASAT	Antisatellite
ASW	Antisubmarine warfare
BMD	Ballistic missile defense
CEP	Circular error probable
C3I	Command, Control, Communications, and Intelligence
CSCE	Conference on Security and Cooperation in Europe
CTBT	Comprehensive Test Ban Treaty
DoD	Department of Defense
FBS	Forward-based systems (principally aircraft)
GCD	General and complete disarmament
GLCM	Ground-launched cruise missile
ICBM	Intercontinental ballistic missile
INF	Intermediate-range nuclear forces
IRBM	Intermediate-range ballistic missile
JCS	Joint Chiefs of Staff
kt	Kiloton (1000 tons)
LTBT	Limited Test Ban Treaty
MIRV	Multiple independently targetable reentry vehicle
MRBM	Medium-range ballistic missile
mt	Megaton (1,000,000 tons)
MX	Missile experimental
NATO	North Atlantic Treaty Organization
NTM	National technical means (of verification)
R&D	Research and Development
SAC	Strategic Air Command
SALT	Strategic Arms Limitation Talks
SCC	Standing Consultative Commission
SDI(O)	Strategic Defense Initiative (Organization)
SLBM	Submarine-launched ballistic missile
SNDV	Strategic nuclear delivery vehicle
SRAM	Short-range attack missile
START	Strategic Arms Reduction Talks

About the Author

Coit Blacker came to Stanford in 1977 as a research fellow with the Arms Control and Disarmament Program. Since then both have taken on new dimensions: The Arms Control Program has become the Center for International Security and Arms Control and Coit Blacker currently serves as its associate director. As Acting Associate Professor of Political Science, he also teaches courses on U.S. and Soviet national security policies and, with Professor John Lewis, on arms control and disarmament.

Professor Blacker's interest in international relations was awakened in his undergraduate years at Occidental College and fully developed by the time he obtained his Ph.D. at the Fletcher School of Law and Diplomacy at Tufts University. It was during his years (1975–1977) as a graduate student fellow at the Harvard Center for Science and International Affairs that his focus became fixed on U.S.-Soviet relations and nuclear arms control. His strong interest in Soviet life and politics has led him to travel frequently to the Soviet Union and to China and to pursue the study of the Russian language.

As a Council on Foreign Relations International Affairs Fellow in 1982, Professor Blacker served on the staff of Senator Gary Hart as special assistant for nuclear arms control. He has published widely for both academic and general audiences and, with Gloria Duffy, was co-editor of *International Arms Control: Issues and Agreements*, published by the Stanford University Press in 1984.

A native Californian, "Chip" Blacker shares his Palo Alto home with Dugan, "the talking horse," a ferocious but lovable giant Schnauzer.

Index

ABMS (anti–ballistic missiles), 106, 125, 167, 173; around Moscow, 37, 44–45, 95, 96, 104, 154; U.S. network of, 96, 104–105, 154, 169

ABM treaty (1972), 3, 37, 106–107, 108, 109, 116, 118, 125, 127, 152, 162, 166, 168, 169, 170, 173

Afghanistan: rivalry over, 19; Soviet Union and, 21, 49, 102, 119, 121, 150

Africa, 5; Soviet involvement in, 102, 119, 121

Alamogordo, New Mexico, 25

Albania, 61, 76

Allende, Salvador, ouster of, 48

Allies, postwar disagreements among, 57–62, 65, 76

Andropov, Yuri, 133, 143, 155, 157, 164

Angola, 20, 115, 129

Anti-ballistic missiles, *see* ABMs

Arab-Israeli conflicts, U.S. and Soviet policies toward, 48–49, 114–115, 116

Arms control: and containment policy, 54–55; as core of detente, 101–102, 104–109, 116–129; future of, 174–175; impasse on, 155–156; negotiations for, 82–84, 96–97, 145–147, 155–156, 161; and nuclear proliferation, 3, 95, 161–162; obstacles to, 162–173. *See also* SALT I; SALT II; START

Arms control agreements, 3, 55, 84, 94, 99; and compliance problems, 169–174; maintaining, 173–175

Arms race, 3, 30; acceleration of, 77, 86, 89, 95, 96, 132–134, 137–138, 142, 161–162; and containment policy, 54–55

Asia, 5, 33

Asia, Southeast, 5, 95

"Assured destruction" strategy, 43, 45, 46, 87–88, 95, 106

Atomic bomb: development and power of, 27, 28; vs. hydrogen bomb, 29

Atomic Energy Commission, U.S., General Advisory Committee (GAC) of, 28, 29

Australia, 47

Austria, sovereignty of, 76

Austrian State Treaty, 76

Axelrod, Robert, 11

Backfire bomber, 117, 120

Balance of power, 7

Ballistic missile systems, 30–40, 82. *See also* ICBMs; Missiles; SLBMs

Basic Principles of Relations (1972), 108–109, 110–111, 114, 128

Bay of Pigs, 53, 91–92

Belgium, 145

Benelux (Low) countries, 10, 65

Berlin blockade, 5, 19, 67, 69

Berlin crises, 46, 80, 84, 92

Berlin Wall, 92

Bernstein, Barton, 3

Bhagavad Gita, 25

Bipolarity, 20, 66; in Cold War, 79–80; dangers of, 8–9, 19, 21; in Europe, 76

Bolshevik regime, 10

Bombers: in delivery system, 30, 32, 34, 36, 45, 86, 137, 151; SALT I, 104, 117; SALT II, 120, 172; START, 147, 148

Brandt, Willy, 21

Brezhnev, Leonid, 5, 99, 108, 112, 119, 120, 128, 133, 134, 144, 163, 164

British Empire, 16, 57

Brzezinski, Zbigniew, 6, 102

Bulganin, Nikolai, 50, 77

Bulgaria, 47, 61, 76

Carter, Jimmy, 6, 36, 136, 140; and detente, 99, 102, 116–128 passim, 136, 145

Castro, Fidel, 48

Central America, 5, 150

Chernenko, Konstantin, 133, 144, 157, 159

Chiang Kai–shek, 72

Chile, U.S. and Soviet policies toward, 48

China: "fall" of, 69–70, 72; and Korean War, 71, 72; and Soviet Union, 21, 85, 103; and U.S., 14, 69–70, 76, 96, 103, 119, 103

Churchill, Winston, 57, 61, 62

CIA (Central Intelligence Agency), 91, 150

Clark, William, 158

Cold War, 3, 115, 134; and arms control negotiations, 82–84; impact of, 53–56, 80; mutual acceptance of bipolarity in, 79–80, 81; origins of, 56–62; Soviet policies during, 55–56, 63, 65–67, 75–77, 79–97 passim; U.S. policies during, 53–55, 63–65, 69–75, 79–97 passim

Communism: fear of spread of, 20, 21, 71, 72; vs. Nazism, 18; Reagan's view of, 136
Concert of Europe system, 49
Conference on Security and Cooperation in Europe (CSCE), 112
Containment policy, U.S., 54, 55, 64–65, 72–73, 102
Crimean War, 7
Cruise missiles, 34–36, 145, 149
Cuba, 17, 20, 22, 50, 115, 121
Cuban missile crisis, 5, 22, 31, 48, 53, 88, 92–95, 103
Cultural Determinism, 11–14
Czechoslovakia, 47, 61, 63, 67, 76; invasion of, 3, 53, 85, 96–97

Detente, 80; and arms control, 101–102, 104–109, 116–129; assessment of, 100–102, 122–129; decline of, 50, 99, 101–102, 114–122, 129; and "linkage" politics, 109, 113–114; opposition to, 99–100, 116–119, 121–122, 132–133, 135; political, 114–116, 127–129; rise of, 77, 101, 102–114
Determinism: cultural, 11–14; historical, 10–11
Deterrence, 2, 42–46, 95, 139–140, 143, 176; minimum, 86–88; mutual, 106; "sufficiency" posture of, 104, 125
Deuterium, 28
Disarmament, 175; proposals for, 55–56, 82. See also Arms control
Drell, Sidney, 175
Dresden, fire bombing of, 27–28
Dulles, John Foster, 20–21, 74
Dyson, Freeman, 2

Eden, Anthony, 77
Egypt, in Middle East conflicts, 80, 114–115
Eisenhower, Dwight D., 21, 30, 71–86 passim; New Look policy of, 53, 75, 131
Estonia, 61
Ethiopia, 102, 129
Europe, 5, 14, 25, 33, 47, 112, 146; bipolarization of, 76; interwar years in, 7
Europe, Eastern, 17, 21, 48, 63, 69, 76, 103; defense of, 47, 55; as postwar problem, 57, 58–62, 65, 66, 67. See also Warsaw Pact Organization
Europe, Southern, 66
Europe, Western, 17, 22, 48, 63, 66; defense of, 47, 89–91, 140, 145–146. See also NATO

Far East, 25, 145
Faure, Edgar, 77
Finland, 66, 67
Fission weapons, 27, 28, 29
Ford, Gerald, 108, 114, 118, 132

Forsberg, Randall, 147
Fourteen Points, 15
France, 7, 10, 17, 50, 59, 65, 80, 81, 85, 92; communism in, 62, 63, 66
Fusion weapons, 28–29

Gaddis, John Lewis, 3, 15
Geneva summit: of 1960, 84; of 1985, 5, 50, 77, 80, 158–159, 165
German Democratic Republic, 47, 69, 76, 84, 92
Germany, 7, 18, 56, 132; as postwar problem, 57–60, 62, 66, 67, 69, 76; and Soviet Union in World War II, 110–11, 41, 57
Germany, Federal Republic of, 7, 17, 19, 69, 76, 125, 145, 155; and Soviet Union, 21, 84
GLCMs (ground–launched cruise missiles), 145
Gorbachev, Mikhail, 5, 50, 133, 158, 159, 164
Great Britain, 10, 11, 62–63, 67, 81, 82; and postwar territorial problems, 57, 59, 60; rivalry with Imperial Russia, 19–20
Greece, 19; U.S. aid to, 63, 65
Gromyko, Andrei, 157

Haig, Alexander, 158
Helium, 28
Hiroshima, atomic bombing of, 27, 28, 55
Historical Determinism, 10–11
Hitler, Adolf, 7, 57, 60; megalomania of, 17–18
Hobbes, Thomas, 6
Hoover, Herbert, 72, 131
Hotline, 94, 103, 126, 157
Hungary, 47, 61; uprising in, 48, 53, 76, 80, 81
Hydrogen bomb, development and power of, 28–29

ICBMs (intercontinental ballistic missiles), 30–37 passim, 43, 45, 86, 87, 89, 96, 138, 142, 151, 174, 175; SALT I, 105, 107, 108, 116–118; SALT II, 120, 124–125, 126, 170, 172; START, 147, 148, 149, 150
Ideological imperative, 14–18, 20–22
India, 21
Individuals, as central actors in international affairs, 9–10
INF (intermediate-range nuclear forces) negotiations, 145–147, 157; collapse of, 155, 157, 158
Interim Agreement (1972), 107–108, 109, 117, 120, 124, 127, 132, 162, 166, 170, 173
International rivalry, 6–8
Iran, 67
"Iron Curtain," 62

Israel: in Middle East conflicts, 48–49, 114–115, 116; U.S. and Soviet policies toward, 48–49, 80–81, 114–115, 116
Italy, 64, 82, 145; communism in, 62, 63, 66

Jackson, Henry, 108
Japan, 10, 19, 62, 67; and U.S., 14, 47, 167
Jefferson, Thomas, 15
Jervis, Robert, 9
Johnson, Lyndon B., 21, 25, 84, 95, 96, 97, 104, 105

Kennan, George, 3, 70; and containment doctrine, 64–65
Kennedy, John F., 22, 25, 30, 42, 83–95 passim, 131, 157; foreign policy of, 85
Khrushchev, Nikita, 5, 16, 21, 50, 75, 76, 77, 84, 85, 89, 92; and Cuban missile crisis, 22, 31, 48, 92–95
Kissinger, Henry, 6, 97, 103, 104
Korea, North, 17, 22, 71
Korea, South, 17, 22, 47, 71
Korean Airlines disaster, 150, 154–155
Korean War, 5, 17, 19–20, 22, 49, 53; significance of, 71–72
Kosygin, Alexei, 95, 96, 105
Kurchatov, I.V., 25

Latin America, 5, 47, 81
Latvia, 62
Laxalt, Paul, 138
Lenin, V.I. 10, 15
Lilienthal, David E., 29
Limited Test Ban Treaty (1963), 53, 83, 84, 94, 103
Lithuania, 62
London Poles, 60, 61
"Lublin Poles," 60

MacFarlane, Robert, 158
McNamara, Robert, 25, 42, 86, 87; 88, 95, 96, 171
Malenkov, Georgi, 75–76
Mao Tse-tung, 69, 72, 76
Marshall, George, 63
Marshall Plan, 53, 63
Marxism-Leninism, 18, 115–116, 136
Massive retaliation, 41, 53, 74–75
Middle East conflicts, 17; U.S. and Soviet policies in, 48–49, 80–81, 114–115, 116
Minuteman missiles, 33, 36, 43, 45, 86, 107, 117, 138, 148
MIRVs (multiple independently targetable re-entry vehicles), 33, 36, 107–108, 121, 124, 150, 170, 174
"Missile gap," 30, 53

Missiles: accuracy of, 43, 117; development and deployment of, 29–37, 43–44, 45, 81–82, 86–87, 104, 120; tests of, 170–171. See also Ballistic missiles systems; ICBMs; SLBMs
Morgenthau, Hans, 6
MPS (multiple-protective shelters), 138
MX missiles, 36, 37, 43, 45, 124, 126, 138, 175, 176

Nagasaki, atomic bombing of, 27, 28, 55
Nasser, Gamal Abdel, 80, 81
National Security Study Memorandum 3, 104–105
NATO (North Atlantic Treaty Organization), 17, 22, 72, 76, 85, 89, 103, 112; "Finlandization" of, 145; "flexible response" doctrine of, 90–91; significance of, 69; U.S. commitment to, 47, 89–91, 145–146
Nazis/Nazism, 7, 10, 59, 60; vs. communism, 18
Negotiations: nature of, 50–51, 53, 162; disarmament, 56
Netherlands, 145
Neutralism, 20, 21
New Look policy, 53, 73, 131
New York Literary Herald, 10
Nicaragua, 20
Nitze, Paul N., 70, 117
Nixon, Richard M., 5, 6, 14, 30, 73, 80; and detente, 97–104 passim, 108, 112, 115, 118, 123, 125, 127, 128, 132, 163
"No-cities doctrine," 86–87
Non-aggression pact, Soviet-German, 10–11
NSC-68 (National Security Council document), 70–71, 73, 117
Nuclear arsenals: bombs, 1, 18, 25, 28, 29, 65, 70, 77; delivery vehicles, 29–37, 77, 86–89, 104, 106, 107, 116–118, 121, 125. See also Arms race; Nuclear weapons
Nuclear freeze movement, 147–148
Nuclear parity, 104, 105, 116, 146
Nuclear tests, 25, 27, 28, 29, 62, 69–70, 77; See also Test–ban negotiations
Nuclear war: agreements on prevention of, 112, 114, 126; brevity of, 1, 6, 25; devastating effects of, 26, 164; resistance to reality of, 26; and "risk averse" pattern, 51
Nuclear weapons: vs. conventional weapons, 1, 27; development and power of, 27–29; impact on U.S.–Soviet relations, 1–2, 46, 49–51, 53–56, 71–72, 74–75; and minimum deterrence, 86–88. See also Arms race; Nuclear arsenals
Nuremburg trials, 60

Credits

The following material has been reproduced with the kind permission of the individuals and organizations listed.

Page

xiv   *Disarmament Talks* © Ralph Steadman.

4   Drawing © 1977 Brad Holland.

24   Poster originally published in the exhibition catalog *Images for Survival* (Washington, D.C.: The Shoshin Society, Inc., 1985).

32   Department of Defense photograph, courtesy *Soviet Military Power 1984*.

44   U.S. Air Force photograph, courtesy the Natural Resources Defense Council.

46   Department of Defense photograph, courtesy the Natural Resources Defense Council.

52   Poster originally published in the exhibition catalog *Images for Survival* (Washington, D.C.: The Shoshin Society, Inc., 1985).

58   Photograph courtesy National Archives.

61   Map adapted from Robert D. Schulzinger, *American Diplomacy in the Twentieth Century* (New York: Oxford University Press, 1984).

68   Cartoon used by permission of Walt Kelly Estate. © Walt Kelly.

78   Illustration © Ronald Searle, 1963, courtesy John Locke Studios.

91   Photograph © Stanley Tretick / *LOOK*.

93   Department of Defense photograph, courtesy the John F. Kennedy Library.

98   Poster originally published in the exhibition catalog *Images for Survival* (Washington, D.C.: The Shoshin Society, Inc., 1985).

110   Text of the Basic Principles of Relations reprinted from Blacker and Duffy, eds., *International Arms Control: Issues and Agreements* (Stanford, CA: Stanford University Press, 1983).

113   White House photograph courtesy The Nixon Project.

130   Poster originally published in the exhibition catalog *Images for Survival* (Washington, D.C.: The Shoshin Society, Inc., 1985).

156   Photograph by Terry Arthur, the White House.

160   Poster originally published in the exhibition catalog *Images for Survival* (Washington, D.C.: The Shoshin Society, Inc., 1985).

165   Cartoon by Kirk Walters, *The Blade* (Toledo).

168   Cartoon by Don Wright, *The Miami News*.

186   Photograph by Chuck Painter, Stanford News and Publications.

The Portable Stanford

This is a volume in The Portable Stanford, a subscription book series published by the Stanford Alumni Association. Portable Stanford subscribers receive each new Portable Stanford volume on approval. Books may also be ordered from the following list.